The Hem of His Garment

True Stories of Healing

Rev. Lawrence J. Gesy, M. Div. M.S.

Our Sunday Visitor Publishing Division
Our Sunday Visitor Inc.,
Huntington, Indiana 46750

ISBN: 0-87973-710-7
LCCCN: 95-71711
Cover design by Peggy Gerardot
The cover shows a fresco from the catacomb of Sts. Marcellinus and Peter, Rome, dating from the beginning of the fourth century (also used on page 32).

Printed in the United States of America
710

Contents

Dedication

This book is dedicated to those in the medical
profession and to those in our church communities
who reach out to the sick and the needy.

Special acknowledgment to:
Drs. Nicholas Fortuin and Peter Green and
the medical and nursing staff at Johns Hopkins
Hospital, Baltimore, Maryland;
Dr. Michael Cox at Mercy Medical Center,
Baltimore, Maryland, and St. Joseph's
Hospital, Townson, Maryland;
and the Catholic Healing Ministry
of Baltimore
and
the Catholic Healing Ministry of Virginia.

Father George W. Kosicki, C.S.B.

Foreword

The man Jesus was limited in space and time, which means that not everyone can reach out and physically touch "the hem of His garment." But it is not enough for Jesus to be in one place in one period of time — in Israel in the first century after Christ.

The Father's great plan of mercy is to continue the life of His Son in each and every one of us who receives Him. By His death and resurrection Jesus sends the Holy Spirit to us who receive Him and so continues His life — His Incarnation and Redemption — in and through us.

St. Paul writes of this continued life of Jesus in us:

> I have been crucified with Christ; yet I live, no longer I, but Christ lives in me; insofar as I now live in the flesh, I live by faith in the Son of God who has loved me and given himself up for me (Gal 2:19-20).

This life of Christ in us is *not* the goal of our life, but rather it is the *beginning* of real life. We are to be the presence of

Christ so that those in need can touch the hem of the garment of Christ — in every time and location.

From this perspective the role of healing can be more easily understood. Healing removes the obstacles to the presence of Christ because it occasions conversion of life, forgiveness, and trust in the Lord.

Healing also removed the obstacles to the continued redemptive suffering of Christ in us for the sake of souls. Healing gives the grace to embrace to the cross of Christ. Again, St. Paul writes:

> Now I rejoice in my sufferings for your sake,
> and in my flesh I am filling up what is lacking
> in the afflictions of Christ on behalf of his body,
> which is the church (Col 1:24).

In *The Hem of His Garment* you will read the testimonies of people's healings of various physical and spiritual ills that hindered the presence of Christ in their lives. Their healings freed them from fears and anxieties as they became instruments of God's mercy to those who touched the hem of their garment.

All healing is a gift of God's mercy. It is love in action for people who do not deserve it. You will read of the numerous examples of Divine Mercy in the testimonies of those who witness to their healing.

God's plan for us is to have mercy on all (see Romans 11:32).

Father George W. Kosicki, C.S.B.
Administrator of Divine Mercy International

Introduction

I have come to understand that there are many kinds of healing. The most important is spiritual healing, complete trust in God's love and mercy, the key to our faith. You will notice a thread that runs through this entire book and its stories: Divine Mercy. I believe that the message of Divine Mercy given to Blessed Sister Faustina is a message of God's power working in the world today. This is why I have included teachings on Divine Mercy in this book.

The foundation of spiritual healing is trust and faith in the teaching of Scripture and the traditions and teaching of the church. God does not dwell in a preoccupied heart. "Be still, and know that I am God." "Jesus I trust in you." I am learning this lesson every day. It is the key to allowing God's work to be manifested.

The other kinds of healing include the healing of memories and relationships and the emotions. This, of course, includes spiritual healing. We cannot be at peace with God without being at peace with one another. Often He has to heal us of the hate, resentments, and the hurtful past before we can begin to trust in His love. We have to learn to love one another before we can love God. Often our relationships with our parents and family members can be reflected onto God, the Trinity, and even the Blessed Mother.

When God uses the healing hands of the priest in the Sacrament of Penance He restores our relationship with God and the Christian community. This is one of the many healing powers that He gives to His priests in the sacrament of Holy Orders. Every priest is a healer, and God calls all of His ordained to use His various charisms.

He also calls those who are not ordained to carry out this aspect of their baptismal calling in a non-sacramental way. This involves surrender of our will to God, to allow Him to come into our lives. Often we are afraid to let go because it may demand that we give up our will to God. That is not easy. What will people say? How will it affect our livelihood and friends?

Absolute trust in forgiveness means that we pray for those who hate us or whom we may even hate. When we can pray for someone that we have hurt or who has hurt us we begin to allow God to work in us. Then surrender, trust that God will take care of the relationship, and He does!

I keep balance in my life with a formula: PIES. This stands for the Physical, the Intellectual, the Emotional, and the Spiritual. If one or more of these is out of balance it is necessary to seek the proper professional or specialist in that area. For example, as a cult expert I know that if a youth has a new group of friends and goes through a sudden personality change, something could be wrong. If a person has a serious spiritual problem, it is strongly recommended that one speak to a compassionate and understanding priest. If one has a marriage problem it is best to seek marriage counseling before the damage is irreversible.

It is also necessary that I encourage caution and discernment in seeking professional help. All that glitters is not gold.

Beware of any individual who promises instant answers to all the world's questions or problems. Beware of any movement that wants to take your mind and your free will. More individuals are referred to great doctors, priests, lawyers, police, etc., by word of mouth than anything else. Stop and think. Seek the advice of others before making a decision. Who told you about your doctor, your dentist, an exciting new parish, or a vibrant new priest? A friend. Beware of anyone who tells you to throw away your medicine!

I have seen many miracles in faith and in medicine, including my own; yet balance is key. The Church has always used caution in discerning all extraordinary phenomena including miraculous healings. Miracles exist. They do happen. God gives us miracles in this broken world to strengthen our weak faith.

As far as I'm concerned, every time a sick person leaves the hospital well, or the emotionally-distraught person is calmed by a good counselor, or the guilty forgiven by the Sacrament of Penance, it is a miracle. Life is a miracle. When we are preoccupied by worry or concerns we often fail to see the miracles all around us. God cannot dwell in a preoccupied heart. Let us look for the miracles in our own lives — and give thanks to God, from Whom all blessings flow.

While this book was being written a priest friend of mine had open-heart surgery. His case is being investigated by Rome as a possible cause for the canonizaiton of Blessed Sister Faustina. This is an example of a miracle in our daily life.

Anna L. Marshall

Healing
in the Old Testament

he pictures which most often come to mind when we think of healing in Scripture are from the New Testament: Jesus curing a blind man or a leper, Jesus approaching the man on the mat by the pool of Bethesda, or Jesus weeping outside the tomb of Lazarus, then saying, "Lazarus, come forth!" If we are asked about healing in the Old Testament, we may think of Elijah restoring life to the widow's son or Elisha curing Naaman the leper. One element contributing to our failure to see the topic of healing as often in the Old Testament is that the word occurs infrequently.

A second factor which makes it difficult to find healing as a theme or topic in the Old Testament is a distorted notion of human nature. How often have you heard, "But that's just human nature" if a youth skips school, or a workman brings home a tool from the job, or someone runs off with another's spouse?

People come in all kinds: gentle souls and rowdies, home-bodies and home-wreckers, drunkards and abstainers, thieves and philanthropists, lazy loafers and workaholics, killers and healers. However, no one is *totally* gentle soul, homebody, or philanthropist without bits and pieces of the negative factors also. The very abundance of human characters which we find in the Old Testament, from Adam to the Hasmoneans, with the full spectrum of faults and virtues displayed before us, blinds us in a way from the deeper truth: *What we see in the people of the Old Testament is not human nature, but fallen nature.*

Starting with Adam and Eve, many people mentioned in the Old Testament needed healing of some sort. That is why the Chosen People longed for a Messiah. The good sorts like Noah and Moses and the prophets might have needed only a touch of healing here or there, but the ones like the Pharaoh and Jezebel seem almost hopeless.

In the past, the term "healing" seems to have been applied exclusively to the healing of physical disabilities or illnesses. So it is true that there are not many cures in that sense recounted in the Old Testament. But a limited sense of the word "healing" should not limit our understanding of Scripture.

Modern medicine and recent expansion of our knowledge of the human mind and emotions have expanded our understanding of what makes us tick. In fact, we have come back to a more biblical approach to people, realizing that our thoughts and feelings are affected by our bodies, and those thoughts and feelings, which we think of as our inner selves, in turn strongly influence our bodily health. The Old Testament speaks of souls in the sense of people, living, walking, breathing, eating people, not as separated from the body. The terms "soul" or "man" (generic for human being) or "person" are used synonymously.

Every human being is a gift from God. Life is such a great gift that we cannot even begin to comprehend it. The account of

Abraham and Sarah is found in Genesis in four places: 12:1-9; 15:1-21; 18:15; and 21:1-13. Sarah was, in modern terms, infertile. Many women want children not only because they truly love children but also because children are living expressions of the mutual love between their husbands and themselves. For such a woman, infertility can be a tragedy, even if she considers adopting a child.

In ancient times, it was assumed that women would prepare the meals and make the clothing for their families. However, a woman's real value was generally defined by the children she could bear who would ensure the continuity of the family or tribe. For Sarah, the pain of childlessness was increased because she knew the tribe expected her to give a child to Abraham to be his successor as leader. She saw herself failing as his wife and was made to feel so by others in the tribe.

When God called Abraham to serve Him, He had promised Abraham that, "I will make you a great nation." This seemed impossible as Sarah grew older, coming to the end of her childbearing years and then passing beyond them into the beginning of old age. She surely felt that Abraham was suffering from his lack of a child. She felt keenly that the tribe blamed her for it. Sarah finally did conceive and bore a son, Isaac, the son God had promised.

The Bible tells us nothing of the inner feelings of Sarah as she desired a child, nor her gratitude at her pregnancy and the birth of her child. The entire account emphasizes God's promise to Abraham and Sarah, the fulfillment of that promise with the birth of Isaac, and the promise that from Isaac would come a great nation. Did Abraham and Sarah feel immense gratitude to God? Of course.

Abraham's strong faith is evident, but his heartbreak when he is asked to sacrifice Isaac is mentioned only briefly. Heartbreak and faith are followed by tremendous joy when God changed His command to sacrifice Isaac and gave Abraham the ram as a replacement. Was Sarah aware of this? Did she know that she was about to lose the child she had so desired? The Bible gives us only the bare facts. The purpose of God's healing Sarah's barrenness — the long-range preparation for the messiah — was hidden from both Abraham and Sarah. Abraham's faithfulness to his call and his obedience laid the foundation for the vocation of the people of Israel to continue to carry the promise of the messiah.

Hannah, the mother of the prophet Samuel, was also infertile and conceived only after prayer and sacrifice. Again, the suffering woman gives birth to a son who is chosen for a special vocation. This calls for a response of faith.

Moses was raised as an Egyptian. His upbringing, education, and early life experience were almost entirely Egyptian. We all come to God with our own particular life experiences. In fact, as we grow in knowledge of God, we come to realize that He has arranged for us to have certain experiences (or has permitted them) for some purpose. We may not comprehend the reasons at the time, but understanding may come after many years.

The Bible tells us that as a young man Moses would not tolerate the injustice of an Egyptian overseer beating an Israelite slave. In the household of Pharaoh's daughter, where Moses was raised, slaves were more expendable than animals. Even so, Moses' actions showed that he considered the slaves human beings.

The exodus of the children of Israel out of Egypt is a momentous event in the story of the Chosen People. When people live in total dependence on others they gradually lose the impetus to freedom of thought and personal initiative. People in prison or in concentration camps or taken as hostages relate how they gradually accept whatever they are given by their jailers as acts of friendship. They begin to excuse their jailers, even while they may hate their conditions. This happens because, even unconsciously, we create little islands of respite from stress in our lives. However, what feels cozy is not always healthful for us.

The exodus was a giant step in the process of healing the

damaged minds and emotions of the Hebrew slaves. The Israelites left Egypt, and by a series of miracles found themselves in
the desert. The pursuing Pharaoh and his army had been destroyed.

In time God gave the Chosen People the Ten Commandments, making those commandments part of His covenant with
this people. This was a kind of amendment to God's covenant
with Abraham. The Ten Commandments could be entitled: "How
to live at peace with God and one's fellow humans." In addition
to the commandments, the Hebrews also had laws for offering
sacrifice to God, sin offerings (asking God's forgiveness), offerings expressing need for healing, recognition of God as the
true source of healing, and thanksgiving offerings, generally
for healing received.

Every encounter with God is an occasion for us to choose
life or to choose death, and we often fail to recognize that we
are choosing death because we allow ourselves to be blinded.
This recurring obligation to make hard choices is expressed
beautifully in Moses' message to the Children of Israel before
his death:

> Here, then, I have today set before you life
> and prosperity, death and doom. . . . I call
> heaven and earth today to witness against you:
> I have set before you life and death, the bless-
> ing and the curse. Choose life, then, that you
> and your descendants may live (Dt 30:15, 19).

There are several pairs of text in the Old Testament which
are fascinating. The most famous instances, of course, are the
back-to-back accounts of creation in Genesis (chapters 1-2:4
and 2:5-25). Another pair, though not so obvious, are the books
of Job and Tobit. They can be considered a pair because they
deal with the same subject matter — the need for healing and
God as the only true Healer.

Most commentators state that Tobit is a folktale presenting the Hebrew picture of the ideal marriage and fidelity to the Law. But it is just as true that it deals with a variety of situations which need healing: old Tobit's blindness, his need for money owed him, his son's need for a good wife, Sara's unfortunate loss of husbands, and her need for a good husband. Tobit is an easy book to read. A short story which is perhaps overly simple, it moves quickly, and the whole account is sunny and upbeat.

The book of Job, of course, is well-known, too. It is not easy reading, because the author is trying to find an answer to that most difficult of questions: Why does God permit evil? In particular: Why do bad things happen to good people? The author of Job wrestled with a deep subject. At the end we find ourselves deeper into the problem but with a better appreciation of it, knowing that God is the only solution. The author of Job replies to the author of Tobit, "Yes, God can and does work miracles, but not in every case, not all the time."

Other clues that God was planning to bring healing to His people are the proclamations of the prophets. Prophecies about the longed-for messiah acknowledge the need for healing, healing of the social structure of the Kingdom, healing for the people. They predict that healing will come *in* the messianic era, but sometimes healings will be *signs of* the messianic era.

> I, the LORD, have called you for the victory
>   of justice,
> I have grasped you by the hand;
> I formed you, and set you
>   as a covenant of the people,
>   a light for the nations,
> To open the eyes of the blind,
>   to bring out prisoners from
>   confinement,
> and from the dungeon, those
>   who live in darkness (Is 42:6-7).

The spirit of the Lord GOD is
    upon me,
because the LORD has anointed me;
He has sent me to bring glad tidings to the
    lowly,
to heal the brokenhearted,
To proclaim liberty to the captives
and release to the prisoners,
To announce a year of favor
    from the LORD
and a day of vindication by our God,
to comfort all who mourn (Is 61:1-2).

Covenants

We tend to use the words "Old Testament" and "New Testament" without realizing that "testament" means "covenant." We will begin with God's covenant with Abraham (the two accounts are in Genesis 15 and 17), the beginning of the children of Abraham as God's Chosen People.

God reached out to Abraham, promising to help him to prosper and to protect him. Abraham in turn promised to be loyal and obedient to the one God. This biblical story tells of the covenant that God wants, an exclusive relationship with Abraham and his descendants. It was a step toward reversing the disobedience of Adam, a step toward healing the rift between God and man, and a step toward healing the results of that rift.

Covenants in the ancient world were like contracts between two parties (such as for sale of land or a marriage) or treaties between governments, and like contracts, they could be amended. One such amendment was God's revelation of the commandments, the revelation of the conduct that God required of the human parties to the covenant. The promise to David that the future messiah would be of his lineage was another amendment from God. Later, many of the prophets indicated that God intended His relationship with the people of Israel to be similar to the relationship of husband and wife.

As we can see from the two accounts of the covenant with Abraham in Genesis, whether a covenant was made between two or more human persons or between God and man, the covenant ritual required sacrifice of animals, the best of the flock. This was a sign of good-faith commitment of the parties, and calling on God to witness that commitment. This was so essential that the term for making a covenant was "cutting a covenant" (*karath berith*).

Israel's people had turned to foreign gods and to seeking wealth by any means, including oppression of the poor. They continued the external appearances of religious practice, but that could not atone for sin. When the people of Israel strayed, and forgot the one true God, the term often used by the prophets in condemning these actions was "adultery." Chastisement would turn Israel back to her true Lover, Yahweh. Nowhere is this more evident than in the book of Hosea, the prophet who lived in Israel, the northern kingdom, just before its fall to the Chaldeans in 721 B.C.

The book of Hosea makes it clear that God sees His people as betraying Him as a harlot wife betrays her husband. Just as Hosea could not give up his wife forever even when her behavior was wanton, so Yahweh would not reject Israel, who had been betrothed to Him. God would instead chastise His people as a jealous lover who tries to bring back his beloved to the springtime joy of their first love.

At the beginning of the section on the Sacrament of the Anointing of the Sick, the *Catechism of the Catholic Church* summarizes the Old Testament treatment of illness and healing (CCC 1502). The quoted sentences have been separated in order to emphasize their content. The references from the footnotes in the *Catechism* itself are in parentheses after each sentence.

The man of the Old Testament lives his sickness in the presence of God. It is before God that he laments his illness, and it is of God, Master of life and death, that he implores healing (Ps 6:3; 38, Is 38).

Illness becomes a way to conversion; God's forgiveness initiates the healing (Ps 32:5; 38:5; 39:9, 12; 107:20; cf. Mk 2:5-12).

It is the experience of Israel that illness is mysteriously linked to sin and evil, and that faithfulness to God according to his law restores life: "For I am the Lord, your healer" (Ex 15:26).

The prophet intuits that suffering can also have a redemptive meaning for the sins of others (cf. Is 53:11).

Finally Isaiah announces that God will usher in a time for Zion when he will pardon every offense and heal every illness (Is 33:24).

Anna L. Marshall

The healing ministry of Jesus

2

I f we watch the television news or read the newspapers, the misery of the world is almost overwhelming, enough to make any ordinary person feel as if the world in which we live is like Job's dunghill or the conditions in Israel at the time of Hosea or in Jerusalem at the time of Jeremiah. Is it too much to hope for solutions like those we read about in Tobit? Is Tobit's ending too sunny to be real? We know instinctively that however broken the world may be, there is truth in Tobit and we cling to that hope.

The problem we have with the ills of the world around us is that it is hard to imagine an unbroken world or unbroken people, and harder still to imagine who could possibly heal all that brokenness. We need healing. But we also need a picture of what a healed person is or can be. Everyone knows what it is to have a broken bone; but if we break a leg, we can remember what that leg was like before it was broken, and that makes the cast and the therapy bearable. As did the people of Israel in Old Testament times, we need not only the hope of a messiah who will bring triumph, we also need a model.

Reading the Old Testament is great preparation for reading the Gospels. No one can read the New Testament without being struck by Jesus' healing of the sick and the crippled, raising the dead, casting out evil spirits, and the apostles and disciples doing some of those same things in the early Church. Moreover, all of these things are specifically mentioned in the Old Testament prophecies as signs of the messianic period and as acts of the Messiah.

The clearest difference between the Old and the New Testaments in regard to miracles and/or healings is that almost all of the signs and wonders in the Old Testament involve natural creation, while most of the special wonders in the New Testament involve human beings.

Prophecy

Jesus Himself chose a prophecy which shed great light on His roles as Messiah, Savior, Healer. After Jesus' baptism in the Jordan River by John, and His retreat and temptation in the desert, Jesus returned to Galilee. Luke's Gospel tells us that Jesus came to Nazareth, where He entered the synagogue on the sabbath, and stood up to read. This is the beginning of His public ministry:

> He stood up to read and was handed a scroll
> of the prophet Isaiah. He unrolled the scroll
> and found the passage where it was written:
> "The Spirit of the Lord is upon me,
> because he has anointed me to bring glad
> tidings to the poor.
> He has sent me to proclaim liberty to captives
> and recovery of sight to the blind,

to let the oppressed go free,
and to proclaim a year acceptable to the
Lord" (Lk 4:15-19).

In this quotation from Isaiah Jesus clearly defines Himself and states the theme of His mission: "Rolling up the scroll, he handed it back to the attendant and sat down, and the eyes of all in the synagogue looked intently at him. He said to them, 'Today this scripture passage is fulfilled in your hearing' " (Lk 4:20-21). The Scripture passage Jesus refers to is from Isaiah 61:1-2.

Two themes of prophecy converge at the beginning of Jesus' public ministry, and both themes are found in Isaiah. The book of Isaiah presents a vivid picture of the hoped-for messiah and his reign. "Messiah" means "the anointed one," which originally meant the king, who was anointed on the day of his coronation. Some chapters prophesy a strong, victorious king, the "son of David" for whom the Jews hoped and prayed.

During the time that John the Baptist was preaching, the people of Judea and Galilee were suffering under Roman rule. It was especially bitter being a subject people for over three hundred years, particularly when they believed they had been chosen by God. The preaching of John the Baptist emphasized the day of the Lord, not a literal day of twenty-four hours, but a moment of time in which God's judgment against sinners will become evident through some severe chastisement.

Many of the Israelites, or Jews, were looking forward to a strong king, the son of David, who would be a kind of arm of God, winning victory against their Roman conquerors and restoring Israel's glory. The day of the Lord would be a day of military victory. But a soldier-king messiah, like David, could have healed only the superficial problems besetting the Chosen People.

The verse from Isaiah (40:3) which refers to John the Baptist is from a section called "The Book of Consolation," starting with the words: "Comfort, give comfort to my people, says your God. . . ." The chapter continues indicating that those words of comfort apply to the children of Israel who have turned back to God after a period of chastisement, which is a preparation for the coming of a messiah who will usher in a period of peace and prosperity.

In the part sometimes called "Second Isaiah" (chapter 40 to the end) are chapters which are known as the "Servant Songs," depicting a different kind of messiah, "the Suffering Servant," one who would suffer greatly for and even from his people. Some of those chapters are very clear foreshadowings of the sufferings and crucifixion of Jesus, particularly Isaiah 52:11-53:12, which is usually read during Holy Week.

In Matthew 11:2-5 we read of the delegation sent to Jesus by John while he was held captive in Herod's prison: "When John heard in prison of the works of the Messiah, he sent his disciples to him with this question, 'Are you the one who is to come, or should we look for another?' "

Jesus said to them in reply, "Go and tell John what you hear and see: the blind regain their sight, the lame walk, lepers are cleansed, the deaf hear, the dead are raised, and the poor have the good news proclaimed to them." Jesus responds to John by listing those works which exemplify the other picture of the messiah and the time of salvation from the prophecies of Isaiah. The works that Jesus summarizes in his message to John in Matthew 11:4-6 are recounted in greater detail in Matthew chapters 8 and 9.

Jesus then gives us a picture of the attitude of some of the people toward His works, His miracles, His healings. He depicts the people as contrasting Himself and John. John comes to them in severely penitential style, while Jesus eats and drinks with the people. Jesus continues in Matthew 11:19: "But wisdom is vindicated by her works."

Even though God does not appear to heal in every case, *the power to create includes the power to restore*, so hope is a necessary next step after faith. Frank Sheed, who had met such thinking in his Catholic Evidence Guild work, summarizes it:

> In the first half of this century especially, expressing belief in the possibility of miracles brought knowing smiles if not scorn from people who had been educated in the sciences. Few people would so radically reject the possibility of miracles as did Thomas Jefferson, who literally cut out of the New Testament every episode recounting a miraculous or supernatural happening. A more common response to the topic of Jesus' miracles is to explain them as natural cures of illness or disability which were not understood at that time, for example that mental illness was mistakenly called possession, that someone in a deep coma was mistakenly diagnosed as dead, that psoriasis or acne was mistaken for leprosy.
>
> . . . Those who accept the miracles but are bothered by the violation of natural laws and wonder why Christ saw fit to work them are under a double confusion. The laws of nature have their own sacredness, of course, but the notion that the Creator is in some way bound by them is almost comic. And in fact a miracle no more violates the laws of nature than a fieldsman violates the law of gravity by catching a ball on its way to the ground. He has simply brought into action another law. That is what God does: he wills to intervene in some decisive way, bringing a new force to bear either to prevent the normal effect of the laws we are all accustomed to count upon, or to bring about some effect beyond what the customary laws

> could by themselves produce. . . . God who cre-
> ated nature with its laws out of nothing can in-
> troduce a new force at will (*To Know Christ
> Jesus*, Sheed and Ward, Inc., 1962).

Another attitude toward healings or cures is almost a coun-
terbalance to scientific skepticism. This is the attitude, even a
belief, that to withhold judgment about an alleged miracle is a
sign of weak faith, that people who say they have seen or experienced cures cannot ever be mistaken.

The Church does not say that only those cures are real which
have been declared beyond the power of medicine or the normal
healing power of the human body to effect. The Church will
only accept those types as certifiably miraculous, but welcomes
the testimony of many whose healing is vouched for by themselves and their friends.

The second reaction to cures is one of determined credulity,
as if withholding judgment about specific cures is a sign of weak
faith. But the determination to see a miracle in every unexplained
cure makes real faith appear to be irrational. The Church does
not dismiss as not real or not important those cures which have
not been declared beyond the power of medicine or beyond the
ordinary healing power of the human body. Such little miracles
are of great value not only to the persons directly concerned but
also to their families, friends, and acquaintances. They attest to
God's providence. The Church only uses certifiable cures as direct evidence of God's intervention as proofs of the heroic virtue
of persons being considered for beatification or canonization.

But the Church's caution in such matters should teach us
that we too need to be prudent about labeling every cure a
miracle. "Modern theology defines miracle as a phenomenon in
nature which transcends the capacity of natural causes to such
a degree that it must be attributed to the direct intervention of
God," John L. McKenzie, S.J., writes in the *Dictionary of the
Bible* (Macmillan Publishing Co., 1965).

If we do not recognize natural laws or laws of nature, but hold that everything is done by God, then there are no miracles. But how does that square with the many interventions of God in books like Exodus, Deuteronomy, and Joshua?

There are four words used in the Gospels that include some of the meaning which we give to the word "miracle": *signs*; *wonders*; *powers* (or *energies,* because the results are produced by Divine power); and *works,* which is the term Jesus gives to them.

What is our attitude toward healing in general and miracles in particular? They are not the same. Both reverse the brokenness of the world, and both express concretely that God does not give up on His creation. Briege McKenna, known as a healer, has said, "Miracles happen, but healing is a process." So we need to read the message that God sends us through both miracles and healing — the message of hope.

The best way to try to understand Jesus' works, His cures, is to follow Him through a series of episodes in a day.

In the first chapter of Mark we read of a series of works:

When Jesus came to Capernaum with His newly-chosen disciples He entered the synagogue on the sabbath and taught. He healed the man with the unclean spirit (cf. Mk 1:23-27).

Then we read that on leaving the synagogue he entered the house of Simon and Andrew with James and John, where He is told that Simon's mother-in-law lay ill with a fever. After grasping her hand and helping her up, the fever left her ". . . and she waited on them" (cf. Mk 1:29-31).

The last of the cures related in this chapter is of a leper. "A leper came to him [and kneeling down] begged him and said, 'If you wish, you can make me clean.' Moved with pity, he stretched out his hand, touched him, and said to him, 'I do will it. Be made clean' " (Mk 1:40-41). The cure of this leper echoes the cure of Naaman in the Old Testament (cf. 2 Kgs 5).

There is one kind of illness which Jesus treated quite differently from others. In every instance when He cured lepers, after the cure He tells them to say nothing until they have presented themselves to the priests. This is because there were specific laws regarding leprosy (see chapters 8 and 9 of the Book of Leviticus). The priests would have questioned the lepers about how they were healed, since the priests would have previously declared the leprous persons banned from towns and from regular activities with other people.

Exorcisms

Modern society often finds it hard to believe in the supernatural. Belief in angels and beliefs in evil spirits, Satan, or devils are often considered absurd or even ridiculous. The great advances in our knowledge of psychology have particularly influenced the attitude of the general public in regard to possession, obsession, and oppression. Even some who believe these conditions can exist find the topic embarrassing.

There are no exorcisms to be found in the Old Testament. Many try to explain away Jesus' exorcisms as the Lord accommodating Himself to the beliefs of His times. That notion is unacceptable because it would mean that He was willing to appear to agree with an untruth. Moreover, Jesus Himself clearly indicates more than once that He is aware that some persons who are mute or deaf-mute suffer from a physical disability, while He indicates that others are obsessed or possessed.

Belief in angels — created pure spirits — is a matter of faith. Because angels are pure spirits they are not limited as we are by our bodies. Nor do they depend on senses as we do for information about the material world. They have much greater strength. While they cannot create matter, they need no hands or feet or material instruments to give them greater power over matter than we have. The fallen angels have not lost the advantage that comes from their angelic nature, but it is very important for us to remember that all angels, good or bad, are limited in their use of their power by the will of God.

What, then, is possession? Angels, good or bad, can influence our senses and our intellects. We think of our guardian angels moving us to do good, to think of some good act and then to do it. The devils, or the fallen angels, likewise can influence our thinking, and so stimulate our desires to do those things to which we may already be tempted by our own inclinations. But possession is more than extraordinary temptation.

While there is often a similarity between many diseases of the nervous system and obsession or possession, the evangelists clearly distinguish between them. The Gospels show Jesus healing deafness, dumbness, blindness, paralysis, apoplexy (strokes and/or high blood pressure), and lunacy (insanity or mental illness). Then in other cases, Jesus or the disciples may state that this or that person's condition of dumbness is caused by a demon.

Two such instances of physical disability with no reference to possession are the cures of deafness and dumbness in Mark 7:32-35 and the cure of blindness in Mark 8:22-26.

Did Jesus use some technique in healing or in exorcizing? In every instance of exorcism cited in the Gospels Jesus simply ordered the demons out as He had ordered their leader away when He was tempted in the desert. In the synagogue at Capernaum, Jesus used no incantations, no excessive gestures. It was the ousted demons who made the outcry. In the case of the Canaanite woman who asked help for her daughter, the daughter was not even present (Mt 15:21-28). It was this very simplicity which occasioned the astonishment of those who witnessed the exorcisms: "All were amazed and asked one another, 'What is this? A new teaching with authority. He commands even the unclean spirits and they obey him' " (Mk 1:27).

Some modern commentators attribute to mental illness the actions of the man or men who met Jesus "as soon as he stepped out of the boat" in Gadara (Mt 8:28-34, Mk 5:1-20, Lk 8:26-39). To flee from society, to live among the tombs or in hovels (or in the case of some of our modern homeless in tarpaper shacks or under railroad trestles), to wear no clothes, howling, and gashing themselves with stones are characteristics of persons probably in need of psychiatric care. That this particular man (or men) were diabolically possessed is proved by the words, "What have I to do with you, Jesus, Son of the Most High God? I abjure you by God, do not torment me!" — discerning that the presence of the Divine Person in the man Jesus is beyond human power.

Seeing the pitiful child of God, Jesus commanded "[the] unclean spirit" to leave the man. Jesus asked, "What is your name?" And he (the unclean spirits answering through the possessed man) responded, "Legion is my name. There are many of us." The evangelists tell us that through the mouth of the possessed the devils entreated Jesus not to drive them out of that country "into the abyss," but to send them into the herd of swine that was feeding nearby. Jesus did so, and the entire great herd rushed

The scene above depicts the encounter of Jesus with the woman with the hemorrhage. The woman who had suffered for many years was healed by touching the cloak of Jesus through the power that "had gone forth from him" (cf. Mk 5:25-34).

down the cliff into the sea and were drowned. The swineherds fled into the town, where they reported the exorcism of the possessed man (or men) and what had happened to the swine.

The townspeople came out to see what had happened. The Gospels tell us that they found the man (or men) whom they had been unable to control before, even with chains and fetters, sitting clothed and in his right mind at the feet of Jesus.

The evangelists tell us that the same day, Jesus and His disciples returned to Capernaum. Luke says that a crowd had gathered to welcome him, "for they were all waiting for him" (Mt 9:18-26, Mk 5:21-43, Lk 8:40-56). What can we think of that crowd? Like ourselves, every person there had needs. Even those who had no illness or disability more than likely had a relative or friend with such a need.

Jairus, one of the leaders of the synagogue, approached Jesus and fell at His feet, pleading for Jesus to come to his house where his only daughter, twelve years old, lay dying. The crowd continued to press about Jesus, who with His disciples had to push through the crowd to follow Jairus to his home. Among them was a woman who had suffered from a hemorrhage for twelve years. Mark tells us that she had spent all she had on many physicians and had suffered much from them without any benefit, "but only grew worse."

Raising the dead

While Jesus was still speaking to people from Jairus's house, someone came to tell Jairus that his daughter had died, so that there was now no reason to "trouble the teacher." Mark and Luke tell us that Jesus heard what was being said and said to Jairus, "Do not be afraid; just have faith."

Jairus had previously responded to that call for faith when he asked Jesus, "My daughter is at the point of death. Please, come lay your hands on her that she may get well and live." Raising the dead is the ultimate healing, and of course created the greatest astonishment as well as arousing contrary responses. Again, notice that every evidence of God's presence in the world creates a choice for those who experience it.

In the Old Testament there are two instances of prophets raising the dead: Elisha restoring to life the son of the widow at Zarephath (1 Kgs 17:17-24) and Elisha restoring to life the son of the couple at Shunem, which was near Naim (2 Kgs 4:18-37). In both of these cases, the prophets exerted considerable physical effort in praying for the restoration of life.

In the Gospels, there are three specific instances of Jesus raising the dead: the daughter of Jairus (Mt 9:18-19, 23-26; Mk 5:21-24, 38-43; Lk 8:41-42, 51-56), the son of the widow at Naim (Lk 7:11-17), and Lazarus (Jn 11:1-44). Except for His signs of grief at the tomb of Lazarus, Jesus exhibited no physical effort in these cases, simply uttering the words of command.

Some of those who refuse to believe that Jesus worked miracles argue that the persons whom Jesus appeared to raise from death were really in deep coma. But Jesus Himself refuted that argument when He dallied before going to the tomb of Lazarus. For three days, the family was expected, by Jewish custom, to visit the tomb in order to ensure that the "dead" person was truly dead and not simply in a coma. Coming with His disciples on the fourth day, Jesus proved His power to raise the dead.

Illness, sin, and healing

In the Gospels, Jesus takes two different positions regarding sin and its relation to illness and disabilities and healing. We need to examine both positions.

After the cures of the woman with the hemorrhage and of the leper, and the raising of the daughter of Jairus, Jesus traveled about Galilee, then returned to Capernaum.

Some men brought a paralyzed man on a stretcher for Jesus

to heal. Mark and Luke tell us that there was no way for them to bring the paralyzed man to Jesus because of the crowd. So the men carrying the man on the stretcher went up on the roof, and according to both Mark and Luke, made an opening in the roof by stripping off some of the tiles, and then lowered the man in the stretcher through that hole (Mk 2:3-4; Lk 5:18-19).

We need to try to imagine this scene, the men wanting a cure for their friend on the stretcher, trying to push through the crowd, shouting "Make way! Make way!" The people around the door were equally determined to get closer to Jesus, perhaps to be cured, telling those men to wait their turn and refusing to budge.

Three of the evangelists (Mt 9:2; Mk 2:5; Lk 5:20) explicitly mention the faith of the men who brought the paralytic: ". . . When Jesus saw their faith, he said to the paralytic, 'Courage, child, your sins are forgiven.' " (Mt 9:2).

Why is this incident in the Gospels? And why did Jesus forgive the sins of the paralytic first, before curing him? Jesus surely knew how the scribes and the Pharisees would react to that? It is probable that Jesus was forcing the scribes and the Pharisees to confront their own attitudes toward sins, illness, the power of God, and who knows what else. Does it take greater divine power to part the Red Sea or to forgive sin?

Matthew tells us that the crowds who saw the cure were "struck with awe, and glorified God who had given such authority to human beings." Mark says ". . . they were all astounded and glorified God, saying, 'We have never seen anything like this.' " Luke tells us, "Then astonishment seized them all and they glorified God, and, struck with awe, they said, 'We have seen incredible things today' " (Lk 5:26).

Have you ever wondered what you would do if you were present when some extraordinary healing occurred? Have you ever experienced an earthquake or a tornado? We think of healings as good and of earthquakes and tornados as destructive, therefore bad. Bad or good, their initial effect on us is surprise, followed by wonder (How did this happen?), followed by fear (What power brought this about?), followed by awe (This surely was caused by very great power!), ending with either more fear, in the case of destructive natural events, or with fear mixed with praise and thanksgiving in the case of the good.

Clearly, Jesus links sin, as a disability of the soul in need of healing, and bodily illness, also in need of healing, and His power to heal both is the same divine power.

A different response of Jesus toward sin and healing is shown in the Gospel of John (9:1-5). In this incident Jesus makes it clear that the pardon He granted the paralytic at Capernaum did not indicate that He was identifying sin as the cause of physical illness or disability.

On a previous visit to Jerusalem Jesus had cured a sick man at the pool of Bethzatha (or Bethesda) on the sabbath. The sick man had been waiting by the side of the pool for someone to help him into the water when it would be stirred, since tradition held that people could be healed at such times. Jesus had told him to pick up his mat and walk. The man was cured at once, but since it was the sabbath, Jews were not permitted to carry such items. Later Jesus sought him out, telling him, "Look, you are well; do not sin any more, so that nothing worse may happen to you" (Jn 5:14). When the man had told the Jewish officials that it was Jesus who had cured him, the Gospel tells us that they began to persecute Jesus for curing on the sabbath. Jesus' reply was, "My Father is at work until now, so I am at work" (Jn 5:17). Again Jesus healed on the sabbath when He healed the man who was blind from birth (read John 9:16).

The healings which Jesus calls works are a kind of replication and extension of the Father's work of creation. Jesus made a mud of clay and put it on the man's eyes, then told him to wash in the pool of Siloam. That mud which was used to heal echoed the creation of man (Adam) from the earth (*Adamah*, the Hebrew word for "earth" [Gn 2:7]).

"Signs" is another word used in connection with healings in Scripture. Signs always indicate something or point to something. What are these signs? To what do they point?

The Gospel according to John was very carefully designed around seven signs. After describing the wedding at Cana in Galilee at which the water was changed into wine, he says, "Jesus did this as the beginning of his signs. . . ." (Jn 2:11); ". . . the second sign Jesus did. . . ." is the cure of the nobleman's son (Jn 4:43-54); the third is the cure of the sick man at the pool of Bethzatha (or Bethesda); the fourth is the multiplication of the loaves and fishes (Jn 6:5-15); the fifth is the cure of the blind man (Jn 9:1-41); the sixth is the resurrection of Lazarus (Jn 11:1-44); and the seventh was after Jesus' resurrection, the miraculous catch of fish after the apostles caught nothing and Jesus told them to let down their nets on the other side of their boat (Jn 21:1-23).

There are many cures or healings mentioned in the Gospels, some without any details recounted, some multiple or "great numbers" of cures, others specifically cures of the blind, or the deaf, or casting out of devils. Each cure or healing, however, is a sign, always and specifically, that God is in our midst, that God is touching us, the Creator restoring His creation. But there is something else. To what are we restored? To what do the signs point?

As we examine episodes in the Gospels when Jesus was healing, what shines through? The disciples and the crowd are seeing God at work, but what else? God seemingly cannot stay away from His creatures. God became man, one of us, not only to die for us on Calvary, but He was willing to put up with thirty-some years of people, many of whom gave no thought to His Father most of the time and many others who filled their lives with breaking His laws.

When we come to the Last Supper that Divine desire to stay with us reaches a zenith. We really need to read and reread often the Scripture texts describing Jesus' institution of the Holy

Eucharist (Mt 26:26-28; Mk 14:22-24; Lk 22:19-20; 1 Cor 11:23-25).

After Jesus broke the bread, He gave it to His disciples saying, "This is my body, which will be given for you; do this in memory of me" (Lk 22:19). Then He took the cup, gave thanks, and gave it to [the disciples] saying, ". . . for this is my blood of the covenant, which will be shed on behalf of many for the forgiveness of sins" (Mt 26:28).

How does the God-man, Jesus, describe to His disciples what this new covenant will bring about? What new relationship between God and His people is being formed? And, above all, what does this have to do with healing?

The Church Fathers saw in Jesus a new beginning for all persons, calling Him "the new Adam." This new Adam, unlike the first Adam, states over and over that He comes to do the will of the Father, and teaches us to say in prayer, "Your will be done, on earth as in heaven" (Mt 6:10). There is the beginning of healing for all humanity.

But, to what does this healing lead? The life of the healed person is described in what is ordinarily called "the discourse after the Last Supper," John, chapters 13 through 17. These passages from Scripture should be read thoughtfully while meditating on Jesus' commandment: "Love one another as I love you" (Jn 15:12).

For centuries the Jewish people had prayed, "Lord, let your face shine upon us," and "Show us your face and we shall be saved." Jesus is truly "the Face of God." God, the Blessed Trinity, whose Being is pure spirit, of course has no face and the prayer of the Jews could be more truly understood as asking for God to favor them in various ways. But in strict truth, when the second Person of the Blessed Trinity became man, the God-man, Jesus, God acquired a face. And since the Blessed Trinity, Father, Son, and Holy Spirit, cannot be separated but, as we can see from what Jesus says here, always act together, the face of Jesus is God's face toward the world He created.

What follows directly impacts the Church, the new people of God and the Mystical Body of Christ: "Amen, amen, I say to you, whoever believes in me will do the works that I do, and will do greater ones than these, because I am going to the Father. And whatever you ask in my name, I will do, so that the Father may be glorified in the Son. If you ask anything of me in my name, I will do it" (Jn 14:12-14).

This is truly the Church's charter: to do the works of healing which we have seen Jesus doing. Down through the centuries the Church in her members has reached out to all in love, and that love has always included the desire to bring healing to the poorest of the poor, the least of Job's descendants. We can see it in the words of the people of ancient Rome who were astounded to "see how these Christians love one another."

In John 14, the charge is given to the apostles not so much as a commission but rather as a statement of fact, that they will, indeed, do these works of love. In several places in Matthew's Gospel, however, Jesus is shown first training the apostles for the work they will be doing, then after His resurrection, giving them the direct commission:

> Then he summoned his twelve disciples and gave them authority over unclean spirits to drive them out and to cure every disease and every illness. . . . "As you go, make this proclamation: 'The kingdom of heaven is at hand.' Cure the sick, raise the dead, cleanse lepers, drive out demons. Without cost you have received; without cost you are to give" (Mt 10:1,7-8).

> So they went off and preached repentance. They drove out many demons, and they anointed with oil many who were sick and cured them (Mk 6:12-13).

The apostles receive their commission to teach only after Jesus' resurrection, after they have been fully instructed by him (cf. Mt 28:20). But the apostles receive more than the promise and commission to heal. The first man and woman had been created in a condition of being able to communicate with God, recipients of His choice favors, managers of His world. The new people of God are now called to an even closer relationship with God (cf. Jn 14:19-21, 23).

Church tradition teaches that the Holy Spirit is the love of the Father and the Son. It is this love, this Person who is love, whom we receive to live with us, and without whom we cannot live the Christian life, with whom we are called, urged, to love all whom God loves. Large order! But anything less is unworthy of the life we have received in baptism (cf. Jn 16:13-15).

When the apostles went out on their mission, they worked various miracles, healed the sick, raised the dead. They were doing as Jesus had foretold, and they were doing these things from their union with the Blessed Trinity: "Amen, amen, I say to you, whatever you ask the Father in my name he will give you. Until now you have not asked anything in my name; ask and you will receive, so that your joy may be complete" (Jn 16:23-24).

We need to grasp strongly the central fact that when Jesus speaks to the apostles He also speaks to us. We, too, are called to that deep union with the Father, the Son, and the Holy Spirit, oneness with the Blessed Trinity. Anything and everything we do must issue from that central fact of our lives or it is worthless and can only result in disorder in our world, as Adam's act of disobedience brought about the mess we live with today.

Notice in John 17:21 that one of the purposes of the unity between persons and between human persons and the Blessed Trinity is "that the world may believe that you sent me." The works done by believers then become signs to lead others into the Kingdom.

Christ's compassion toward the sick and his many healings of every kind of infirmity are a resplendent sign that "God has visited his people" (Lk 7:16, cf. Mt 4:24) and that the Kingdom of God is close at hand. Jesus has the power not only to heal, but also to forgive sins (cf. Mk 2:5-12); he has come to heal the whole man, soul and body; he is the physician the sick have need of (cf. Mk 2:17) " (CCC 1503).

But he did not heal all the sick. His healings were signs of the coming of the Kingdom of God. They announced a more radical healing: the victory over sin and death through his Passover. On the cross Christ took upon himself the whole weight of evil and took away the "sin of the world," (Jn 1:29; cf. Is 53:4-6) of which illness is only a consequence. By his passion and death on the cross Christ has given a new meaning to suffering: it can henceforth configure us to him and unite us with his redemptive Passion" (CCC 1505).

Anna L. Marshall

The Church as healer

esus is present in the world today: in the Holy Eucharist, in His Church, in the Scriptures. But we hope for His coming in final glory. Since we do not know when that will be, and we are certain that some day, probably before that Parousia, we will be called to meet Him in death, the entrance to another life. We look forward to both meetings. That hope, with all its desire for healing, for ourselves and for the whole world and everyone in this life, is a whole way of life that began immediately after the resurrection of Jesus and His ascension to the Father.

Matthew 10 relates that early in Jesus' public life, He not only prepared the apostles for a ministry of teaching and preaching, but also a ministry of healing:

- Verse 1 — "Then he summoned his twelve disciples and gave them authority over unclean spirits to drive them out and to cure every disease and every illness."
- Verse 7 — "As you go, make this proclamation: 'The kingdom of heaven is at hand.'"

• Verse 8 — "Cure the sick, raise the dead, cleanse lepers, drive out demons. Without cost you have received; without cost you are to give."

Here we see Jesus as the new Adam passing on to His disciples power to restore damaged creation, "authority" to "drive out" unclean spirits and to "cure every disease and illness." The first part of verse 8 simply lists the types of cures, but verse 7 provides the setting and the rationale. "The kingdom of heaven" was one of the ways the Jews used to speak of God without using the sacred name, Yahweh, which they were forbidden to speak. So the curing of the sick, raising the dead, cleansing lepers, and casting out devils would be visible proof of their proclamation, "The kingdom of heaven is at hand." Mark (6:12-13) provides the sequel: "So they went off and preached repentance. They drove out many demons, and they anointed with oil many who were sick and cured them."

During that period which the Church celebrates as the time after Jesus' resurrection and before His ascension, Jesus again spoke to the apostles of the Church as healer: "These signs will accompany those who believe: in my name they will drive out demons, they will speak new languages. . . . They will lay hands on the sick, and they will recover" (Mk 16:17-18).

How does the Church follow in the footsteps of Jesus, the Divine Healer? From about the tenth century through Vatican Council II, the sacrament of the sick was called Extreme Unction ("last anointing"), a name or title which led both priests and laity to believe that the sacrament should be received only when a person was in danger of death or actually dying. A clearer understanding of the sacrament is found in the Epistle of James (5:14-15) which clearly indicates the customs of the apostolic period: "Is anyone among you sick? He should summon the presbyters of the church, and they should pray over him and anoint [him] with oil in the name of the Lord, and the prayer of faith will save the sick person, and the Lord will raise him up. If he has committed any sins, he will be forgiven."

How did we get to Extreme Unction from those words? That requires more time and space than we have here, but suffice it to say that we grow in understanding of ourselves as human beings and of the great treasury of truths bequeathed to the Church by Jesus and protected by the Holy Spirit.

That journey through nearly two thousand years of persecutions, wars, religious disputes, and missionary journeys to many lands with countless different languages and cultures brings before our minds the enormous task the Church has always had: both to preserve and defend and also to grow in understanding of the truths she has received from Christ.

"Oil of the Sick" was the common term from the earliest days of the Church until now, and that very name indicates that the sacrament had been understood in a broader sense than one limited to a last anointing (which became the ordinary name only toward the end of the twelfth century). It is significant that through all the changes over time, the old prayers continued to stress alleviation, strengthening, and healing. Even when the sacrament was administered only when a person was in imminent danger of death, the prayers continued to be for restoration of health and a return of the patient to customary activities.

Sulpicious Severus, the biographer of St. Martin of Tours (fourth century), writing shortly after St. Martin's death, tells of numerous miraculous cures obtained by St. Martin through prayer and the use of blessed oil.

St. Cyril, Bishop of Alexandria, writing early in the fifth century, scolds those Christians who resort to pagan healers and customs, urging them to call on their priests for prayer and blessings with oil.

In the fifth century (A.D. 416), Pope Innocent wrote to Bishop Decent of Gubbio (Letters 25, 8) that the Oil of the Sick should not be given to sinners doing public penance since the anointing of the sick was "a kind of sacrament" and penitents were not allowed to receive the other sacraments.

The Oil of the Sick is blessed by the bishop for the use of the

The Church as healer

priests of his diocese, in administering the Sacrament of Holy Anointing at the Chrism Mass on Holy Thursday. The texts of the liturgical prayers used at that blessing include first an exorcism formula that "this oil may have power to effect a spiritual anointing so that the temple of the living God may be strengthened and the Holy Spirit be able to dwell in it."

Second is a solemn blessing, invoking the Holy Spirit: "Lord, we pray you, send your Holy Spirit, the Advocate, from heaven upon the olive oil . . . that it may strengthen soul and body, and that by the power of your holy blessing anyone anointed with this heavenly medicine may be protected in soul and body and be freed of all pain, weakness, and sickness of soul and body."

The blessing of the oil ends with: "As you once anointed priests, kings, prophets, and martyrs, so may the perfect chrism which you have blessed for us continue to work within us."

Commentators on the ritual remind us that the clause "As you once anointed" does not refer to the oil, but to the Holy Spirit, who has just been invoked in the main part of the sentence. "Your perfect chrism" also refers not to the oil, but to the Holy Spirit, "who is the crowning messianic gift to Christ and Christ's saving gift to us" (Adolf Knauber, translated by Matthew J. O'Connell, *Pastoral Theology of the Anointing of the Sick*, Liturgical Press, 1975).

Prayer to saints — praying with saints

Saints have an inside track toward knowing and loving God, so they should be experts at teaching the rest of us, especially about healing. Why emphasize healing? The Church requires that two first-class miracles be obtained by prayer after a person's death before that person can be declared a saint. This would indicate that the person was very close to God.

Sister Thérèse of Lisieux was declared "Blessed" in 1923, then canonized on May 17, 1925, by Pope Pius XI. Before she died, Thérèse had told her Sisters in the Carmel of Lisieux, France,

"I will spend my heaven doing good upon earth. I shall let fall from heaven a shower of roses. My work begins after my death."

In the 1920s and 1930s many pastors invited missionaries to preach missions or novenas in their parishes, introducing their parishioners to the life and virtues of St. Thérèse. When persons received the favors or healings they prayed for during those times of special prayer, Thérèse's "shower of roses" became more widely known. In the years between the two world wars, statues of the Little Flower in her Carmelite habit, holding an armful of pink roses, began to appear in parish churches, donated to them in gratitude for favors received through her prayers.

The 1930s were a period of great Catholic intellectual and spiritual growth in the United States. Mother Frances Cabrini, who had built hospitals and staffed schools for Italian immigrants, had recently died, but the memory of her work and her love of God and His people was still fresh. Mother Katharine Drexel was still alive, and her work for the Native Americans and African Americans was flourishing, as was the renown of her donation of her immense fortune to support it.

My personal experiences of meeting other remarkable women who were dedicated to the Church are first in my memory.

During my college days I became a member of a sodality. Sodality members were supposed to express their love of God in actual works of charity, such as pushing wheelchair patients to Sunday Mass in the city hospitals or working the soup lines or sandwich lines at churches or teaching reading to illiterate adults.

The sodality moderator decided that we needed to learn more about Catholic Action, so one day a woman came to address us. She was the Baroness Catherine de Hueck, foundress of Friendship House in Harlem. She had learned the bitter lesson that the social class to which she had belonged in Russia had seriously failed their obligations to society. The peasants and the poor had turned against them. "The B," as she was called, was imprisoned in her own home until she was liberated by anti-Communist troops.

By the time she came to address our sodality she was living a life of voluntary poverty and service. Her first two Friendship Houses were started in Toronto and Ottawa (1930 and 1936) with a bread line, rooms to distribute clothing, libraries, and discussion groups and clubs. In New York she was starting a third Friendship House in Harlem. Some of us gathered around her in the student lounge to ask questions.

The word "blunt" fit her perfectly. "The B" was shaped like the blocky babushkas seen sweeping Russian streets in news photos. Once past the first impression of babushka and chain-smoker, the next revelation was the way she spoke of God, of Jesus, of the Holy Spirit. "The B" lived with God as you or I might live with our family and friends, totally at home, and totally self-giving to her neighbors. No one could have looked less like a saint, but I caught glimpses of an interesting inner life.

Another place for our sodality works of mercy was the Catholic Worker house in New York's Bowery, founded by Dorothy Day. Having known her in the early days when her work was just starting, I find myself catching my breath in surprise when I read about her now in religious education textbooks. I am not surprised that she is presented as an example of Catholic faith in action. However, I am surprised that while I did and do respect her, she was so very ordinary, even abrasive at times. Somehow the pictures on glossy textbooks pages make her seem unreal, someone I never knew.

During this same period of time, New York was sometimes home to some eminent Catholic writers and publishers, among whom were the Sheeds, better known as Frank Sheed and Maisie Ward. They were making major sacrifices to bring good, up-to-date Catholic writing to the public. At Sunday afternoon forums in their home, the Catholic reading public could occasionally meet some of those authors. Frank and Maisie were as open and unaffected as "The B" and Dorothy Day. They were simply dedicated to what they saw as a vocation, and sincerely giving of themselves.

Is this what sanctity is all about? And what does it have to do with healing? I put those questions to one side and simply noted the experiences.

As World War II came to an end, returning soldiers brought with them reports about an Italian Capuchin priest, Padre Pio, who had the stigmata (the signs of the wounds of Jesus) in his hands, feet, and side. St. Francis of Assisi and a few other saints, most of whom had been cloistered nuns, had also been stigmatists. Padre Pio was the first priest in the history of the Church to be so marked.

At that time, I was beginning to understand that sanctity consists in doing the job at hand, in bringing Christ into the workplace and the home. Besides, if we mean what we say when we say that Jesus is truly present in the Blessed Sacrament, why would we need to go traipsing off to other parts of the world to look for Him in this or that saintly person? But Padre Pio drew my attention, and I began to read everything about him that came to hand. Since Europe was recovering after the war, Italy might as well have been light-years away, as far as considering a visit to see this holy man.

Brooklyn, however, was another matter. Anyone could travel on the subway anywhere within New York City for a nickel. From friends who lived in Ohio and Indiana, I had heard of a Capuchin priest in Detroit who had a reputation for sanctity and healing, Father Solanus Casey (who has just been declared "Venerable," the first American-born man to reach that stage toward canonization).

Father Solanus had been transferred to the Capuchin house in Brooklyn, where he was the doorkeeper, as he had been in Detroit. A friend lived in that parish, so one day after having lunched with her, I made my way to the friary and rang the doorbell. A Capuchin of indeterminate age opened the door.

"Indeterminate" because, although his beard was very gray, his eyes twinkled youthfully. I asked to speak with Father Solanus. To this day, over forty years later, I can hear his reply clearly in memory, even to the tone of his voice: "I have the misfortune to be that miserable sinner."

From almost anyone else those words would have sounded artificial, pretentious, an attempt to appear holy. Almost more shocking than the words was the obvious fact that this Capuchin friar sincerely meant them. I say shocking because in that instant this meeting had progressed from a level of polite inquiry to the deepest level of human being meeting human being in the presence of God. The spiritual shock was almost as palpable as the physical feeling we used to get when an elevator would drop too many floors too quickly.

Father Solanus ushered me to a small parlor, a bare room with a small, plain wooden table, and two very straight, very plain wooden chairs, no carpet, no curtains, all of which was standard Capuchin decor at that time. We spoke about prayer, about desiring to love God more, about working at overcoming faults, but most of all Father Solanus emphasized the Mass — and the importance of not only attending Mass whenever possible — but having Masses offered for not only our own personal intentions, but for God's intentions, such as conversions, here and in mission countries, in what we today would call the Third World.

Everyone who visited Father Solanus was urged to contribute something to the Seraphic Mass Association, the organization through which Capuchin missions were supported and for whose members the Capuchin missionaries throughout the world offered Masses. As often as I met him (several times while he was in Brooklyn) Father Solanus emphasized praying for others as the prerequisite for obtaining the particular favors we might desire.

In the course of a lifetime I have met many lovable people (and some with a few quirks of personality that made liking a bit difficult, but whose love of God and neighbor made loving easy). Each has taught me something about God and about how to grow as His child. This is healing, taking a crooked branch of a vine and bending it to grow in God's way. None of them did it by school-type teaching, nor by obvious directions, but I think of them like sunlight drawing a plant, as people who have helped me to understand the place of saints in the Church.

Over many decades of praying, reading, and living, a person can become accustomed to the teachings of the Church, the liturgy of the Church (in spite of changes), the history of the Church (not dates and events so much as the persons — the saints and sinners who made the history), so that the Church becomes like a house in which one is familiar enough to move at ease even in the dark. The writings of some of the saints become like voices of family members, so that when we read something they have written we recognize the voice of a dear friend or sister or brother.

The Church is called "the Mystical Body of Christ"— St. Paul's term, but the truth of it was shown him by Jesus when He appeared to the former Saul on the road to Damascus. In the light which surrounded him, Saul heard, "Saul, Saul, why are you persecuting Me?"

"Who are you, Lord?" Saul replied.

"I am Jesus whom you are persecuting" (Acts 9:1-7).

Of course, Saul did not think he had been persecuting Jesus, whom he thought was a blasphemer anyway. Saul wanted only to clean out the followers of Jesus from the Jewish community, which he believed should be concentrating on living up to its pure covenant obligations. But here was Jesus before him, obviously alive, and saying that He and His followers were one. To state it simply, Saul (who became Paul) never got over it.

So this Church is not an institution, although it must have certain institutional characteristics in order to function. It is a living body, and if it is the House of God, it is not in the sense of a building, but like a family home, full of diaries of family members, and pictures and artifacts, relics of those through whom our Big Brother, Jesus, carried on His work in the world. It's the family trade. Each of us is called to go out and heal the world for our Father.

The Blessed Virgin, saints, and shrines

Why do we find that praying to saints or near-saints often brings about healing or even miraculous cures? Why do we call some persons "saints"? We see something in the character of those persons which tells us that they are trying to follow Christ. They are willing to go all the way for love of God and neighbor. In the First Epistle of John we read: "If anyone says, 'I love God,' but hates his brother, he is a liar; for whoever does not love a brother whom he has seen cannot love God whom he has not seen. This is the commandment we have from him: whoever loves God must also love his brother" (1 Jn 4:20-21).

Whenever we make the Sign of the Cross we say, "In the Name of the Father, and of the Son, and of the Holy Spirit." When we say the "Glory be . . ." we do the same. When we recite the Creed, the Nicene Creed at Mass or the Apostles' Creed, we proclaim our belief in the Blessed Trinity. We have been thinking about the Father and the Son — not too difficult. But what about the Holy Spirit? The First Letter of John is a hymn to God as Love. This is the God to whom Jesus introduces us when we read the Gospels, and especially when we read the discourse after the Last Supper. There He speaks to us of the Advocate whom He will send when He goes to the Father.

Who is the Holy Spirit? The Love breathed, "spirated," between the Father and the Son. We say there is no difference between the Persons of the Blessed Trinity. Each is true God; the difference, if we dare to use that word, is in their relationships to one another. Since God has told us that He wants to dwell in us and among us, and for this "indwelling" we must grow to "be perfect as your heavenly Father is perfect," just what is that perfection? Love. If we love God and our neighbor we are setting up relationships, bringing the Holy Spirit to dwell in us and to bring God back into His world which was stolen from Him by sin.

In the true stories of healing in this book, we see Divine Mercy at work in many lives, Jesus doing His works in a broken world. All around us, wherever we look, people need healing. Each of us has some part which needs to be healed, some annoying or unpleasant habits which annoy us or those who know us. Some of us have memories that trigger deep emotions which we find hard to shake, or some damaged relationships with members of our families or with neighbors or co-workers. Our communities (whether local or the larger communities of nations) all show need for healing of relationships.

In the writings of some medieval saints, and particularly in the writings of St. Gertrude (d. 1302), we read of Jesus showing Himself to them as the loving Savior with the pierced heart, the Savior explaining that the piercing of His heart after He had died on the cross was symbolic of how His heart had been broken with love for us in spite of our forgetfulness or disdain for God evidenced by our sins. He told St. Gertrude that He would reveal Himself more generally in the future (at the time the devotion was known only to a few monks or nuns), "when the world will have grown cold."

That revelation of the Sacred Heart of Jesus was given to St. Margaret Mary Alacoque in several visions from 1673 to 1675 in France. The "cold" which Jesus had foretold to St. Gertrude was a kind of super-Catholic heresy called Jansenism, which made people fearful of a stern, rigorously just God. (Not that God is not just, but the God who can say, "Father, forgive them, they know not what they do" is a God whose justice does not minimize the sin, but who still sees the guilt of the sinner as lessened by frailty and ignorance.) The people of the seventeenth century needed to see Jesus as the God of the loving Heart and to be drawn by that love.

Reparation to our Savior God, as St. Margaret Mary describes what she had learned from Jesus, is simply loving the God who has been forgotten, ignored, even insulted by flagrant sin, is a way of telling God that we adore Him and love Him, and we desire that we, ourselves, should never again turn against Him by sin, and we desire that all His creatures should respond to His love by obedient love.

Is the revelation of Jesus to Blessed Faustina very different? I think that when we read her writings carefully we discover that the difference is mainly in emphasis. In the writings of Blessed Faustina we see the same loving Savior again asking us to respond to His Love, but now in a world where unspeakable crime is rampant, in the country where concentration camp doctors used innocent people, imprisoned for no reason except their race or religion, for horrible experiments. Jesus shows Himself to a bleeding world as the Savior pleading for us to seek His mercy, and equally to show mercy to our brothers and sisters and to plead that His healing mercy embrace all peoples.

Are there any differences? No, in none of these instances is there a new revelation. It is the same Jesus we saw at Cana, taking pity on the young bride and groom to spare them the embarrassment of running short of wine at their celebration, the same Jesus who wept out of sympathy for Mary and Martha when their brother Lazarus was in the tomb. We sometimes need a new picture of Jesus to remind us of what we should know from the Scriptures and the teaching of the Church.

Is it enough to pray the prayers revealed to Blessed Faustina, to make the Holy Hour of reparation that Jesus requested of St. Margaret Mary, to make the Communions of reparation on the nine First Fridays as He asked of St. Margaret Mary? If a person sincerely prays those prayers, sincerely receives the Holy Eucharist in repentance and love, sincerely makes a Holy Hour of reparation (which is, again, repentance and love), such a person will grow in love of God and love of neighbor, which is the only way to gain Heaven.

But will this apparently simple way of prayer and reparation heal the broken world? "More things are wrought by prayer than this world dreams of." Who knows how much of Peter Claver's work can be ascribed to the prayers of the simple brother, now St. Alphonsus Rodriguez, who stayed home in Majorca and prayed first for Peter Claver to go to the new world as a missionary, and then prayed for his work in Cartagena? There are many other instances like that, but the greatest one is Mary. How much of the good work of the apostles is the result of her prayer for the souls of the persons of her time and all the ages yet to come? She loved and loves all for whom Jesus suffered and died; that is, all of mankind.

Healing begins with love of all whom God has created — and all of their concerns.

> Be doers of the word and not hearers only, deluding yourselves. For if anyone is a hearer of the word and not a doer, he is like a man who looks at his own face in a mirror. He sees himself, then goes off and promptly forgets what he looked like. . . . Religion that is pure and undefiled before God and the Father is this: to care for orphans and widows in their affliction and to keep oneself unstained by the world (Jas 1: 22-24, 27).

What about miraculous cures and healings connected with the Blessed Mother Mary, the Miraculous Medal, and Lourdes, for instance? How do we think about Mary (of Bethlehem and Nazareth, and then probably of Ephesus, where she apparently lived with the Apostle John after the resurrection of Jesus)? Is she like a one-dimensional, holy-card picture in our minds? Is she like a statue? Or do we see her holding Jesus as an infant, then following Him (like a shadow), and holding His Body at the foot of the Cross?

No matter how pure and sinless she was, Mary was sufficiently ordinary in appearance and in action that the people of Bethlehem and later Nazareth took her for granted as one of them. She did not walk about surrounded by light or raised above the ground. But the important thing about Mary is that she always did the will of God. Listen to her words at Cana: "Do whatever He tells you" (Jn 2:5). Tie those into her words to Gabriel: "I am the handmaid of the Lord. May it be done to me according to your word" (Lk 1:38). Later, when Jesus was told that His mother and brothers were outside wishing to speak with Him, He replied, "Who is my mother? Who are my brothers? . . . For whoever does the will of my heavenly Father is my brother, and sister, and mother" (Mt 12:48-50). On another occasion, when a woman praised Jesus by saying, "Blessed is the womb that carried you and the breasts at which you nursed," He replied, "Rather, blessed are those who hear the word of God and observe it" (Lk 11:27-28).

This brings us back to the saints. If a person has not died as a martyr, the Church uses proven first-class cures after death as a yardstick to tell us whether or not a particular individual has met God's standards for heroic sanctity. Cures during their life on earth are not acceptable for that, because each of us has until the moment of death to remain close to God or to reject Him. The saints are people who see the world as it is, broken and severely damaged by sin. Only we, the children of God, can bring it healing.

Should we wring our hands, helplessly waiting for God to send an angel to stir the waters of healing? By our baptism we are brought into a relationship with God, made a child of God, and (in the words of the older catechism) "an heir of heaven." Jesus taught us to say, "Our Father." Jesus, our Brother, came to bring healing love into the world. For two thousand years the saints have followed in His footsteps. Now it is our turn.

What kind of healing can we bring to the world?

Not everyone is called to work as a nurse or a doctor, as a psychotherapist in a mental hospital, or as a counselor for drug or alcohol addicts. It is rare for someone to feel called, as was Father Damien of Molokai, to shut himself off from the company of ordinary people to spend the rest of his life quarantined with lepers.

We saw how Jesus healed lepers. There are many instances of saints who healed lepers. St. Francis of Assisi, for example, was a fastidious, elegant, rich young man. Then he was touched by the grace of Christ, who spoke to him from a crucifix, saying, "Rebuild My Church." Francis misunderstood at first, and started to personally rebuild the little chapel, lifting and replacing the fallen stones. That chapel is called the Portiuncula ("Little Portion," today a special shrine in Assisi). Then he saw a leper coming down the road. Francis found the man repulsive, but he realized that the leper too was a child of God, so repenting of his hesitation, he ran to the leper, and embraced and kissed him. That act of love was sufficient so that God healed the leper. Gradually Francis came to understand that everyone is called to rebuild the Church anew every day, each of us in our own lifetimes.

There were still lepers around in 1873, especially in tropical countries, when young Father Damien de Veuster left Belgium for the Hawaiian Islands. Lepers there were condemned to live on a portion of the island of Molokai that could only be reached by ship. No one could visit them and return to the ordinary world. Love, springing from God's grace, moved Father Damien to choose voluntary exile till death to live among the lepers. That love changed the lepers from bitter, despairing persons (some cursing God, because society wanted to get rid of them) into decent, joyful Christians. That was the healing miracle of Molokai.

Another healing miracle was not necessarily a healing. When a group of Sisters volunteered to go to Molokai, Father Damien told them that none would get leprosy. Father Damien himself had contracted leprosy, which enabled him to become truly one with his flock. Eventually he died of the disease. However, no Sister who worked on Molokai ever contracted leprosy.

Some of those Sisters did the medical research that resulted in the discovery of the medication which effectively cures leprosy today and prevents it from developing into the terribly disfiguring and debilitating disease which people so dreaded in the past.

We see how the love of St. Francis brought forth a miraculous cure, and how the love of Father Damien healed ravaged souls and devastated emotions, bringing faith, hope, and love into spiritual darkness. The love of the Sisters, reaching out and bringing the comforts of good nursing to those who were not allowed in ordinary hospitals, finally resulted in their love reaching for new horizons in medicine to help those abandoned by society. What we may not see — unless someone like Father Solanus has opened our eyes — are all the members of the associations and groups who help the missions by praying for their fellow Christians who work among the lepers and other poor persons in developing countries.

We may know a neighbor who had to drop out of some favorite club because she is caring for a relative with Alzheimers, or is nursing a parent dying of cancer. Do we hesitate to volunteer to spend a couple of hours with the patient? Are we afraid to see the wreck of someone we knew as a healthy, competent person? Are we afraid of seeing how illness can change someone? Are we afraid of a sick person's emotions? What is it we fear? That pity and love may overcome our smooth face to the world?

The story of Veronica is the story of all Christian healers. In a church in Rome there is a piece of cloth, popularly called "Veronica's Veil," which bears the image of the face of Jesus. Veronica is not the name of a woman, but stems from *vera*, Latin for "true," and *eikon*, a Greek word for "image" (true image).

Legend has it that while Jesus was carrying the cross to Calvary, a woman, moved by pity, rushed out from the crowd and wiped His face with her veil, then found the image of His face imprinted on it. The woman, if there was such, was utterly forgetful of self, heedless of public disdain that she was showing sympathy for a condemned criminal. Few healers need such heroic self-forgetfulness.

One who did was St. Peter Claver, who went into the stinking hulks of the slave-traders' galleys in the port of Cartagena to nurse the sick. He would carry the sick on his own back to the poor hospitals for the slaves, where often he was the only one to nurse them. He was severely criticized by officials, by proper society, and even by his fellow religious for getting so close to the dirty, odorous, and probably contagious slaves whom he nursed, but whom no one else seemingly cared about. But Peter Claver saw in them the same bleeding face of Christ that the woman we call Veronica saw on the way to Calvary.

There is another side of Christ shown in the stories of each of these healers. When we see Peter Claver jumping into the holds of slave ships, we see a seventeenth-century Spanish gentleman painting on his soul the image of Jesus, God become man for love of His Father, the Creator whose creatures had turned against Him, but also for love of the creatures, of whom He said, "They know not what they do."

That same bleeding face of Christ calls today to Mother Teresa and her Sisters from the muddy gutters of Calcutta and the slums of other cities throughout the world. The same bleeding face of Christ is everywhere around each of us, in the well-dressed businessman whose daughter has run away from home to live with a rock musician on drugs, in the woman whose husband beats her when he drinks, in the man or woman who has arthritis or emphysema or cancer, in the teacher who tries to impart basic knowledge to children whose parents do not encourage them to learn, and especially in the Christians who are baptized but whose lives are not lived according to their faith. That bleeding face of Christ calls to their pastors, nuns, lay ministers, fellow-Christians of all kinds.

As God told the children of Adam to "be fruitful and multiply; fill the earth and subdue it," (Gn 35:11) giving them the animals and the plants for food, the new Adam, Jesus, calls us as His brothers and sisters to bring that world which He has redeemed back to His Father. Healers need to be gardeners. The parable of the sower (Mt 13:4-9) appears to focus on the kind of ground that received the seed, but Jesus was speaking to farmers and fishermen. They know that soil can be improved. Every farmer knows that digging out rocks can give him additional ground for planting. Pulling up thorns can do the same and watering the ground can increase yield.

Take a moment and read the parable of the sower in the Gospel of Matthew (13:4-9), along with the explanation which the apostles requested from Jesus (18-23). Read also the variant readings from the Gospels of Mark and Luke.

Sacramentals — medals, relics

Medals, relics, pictures, and statues are reminders, but with an added dimension. The added dimension is this: Anything connected with a truly holy person — his or her pens, books, clothing — has been used for good, for doing the will of God, reclaimed for God's service. A medal struck to teach a lesson about God is something separated from worldly use.

The Miraculous Medal is called because so many healings came to be associated with it. If you closely examine the medal or a picture of it you will see that both sides of that medal remind us of some of the foundational truths of our Faith. It deserves more extended space than I can give it here, as do the full stories of the revelations of the Sacred Heart and Divine Mercy. God can touch us, therefore, by way of medals and relics. We do not ascribe any power to them as such except as means which God can and does use. It is because they have been reclaimed for God and because He can use them for our good that the devil has been known to rage against such medals and relics during exorcisms.

Sometimes I have been asked, "How did Jesus heal?" or, "I would like to know how to heal." Those questions arise from a misconception of healing. At the present time many Christian people are influenced in their thinking about the world around them and God's intervention in our world and our lives by the New Age movement and other religions, some even appearing to be quite pious forms of Christianity.

New Age, neo-paganism, witchcraft, and all of those syncretistic religious movements attempt to influence the world around us by manipulation of things or of people. (See Father Larry Gesy's book, *Today's Destructive Cults and Movements,* published by Our Sunday Visitor for further explanations.) Only true faith in the true God can bring about healing.

On television and in articles in newspapers and magazines we often hear or read about persons who *appear* to cure or heal even so-called incurable diseases or defects. That kind of thing was not unknown in Old Testament times as well as at the time of Christ. The priests of the Egyptian religion who challenged the power God gave to Moses, and who seemingly were able to perform some feats of magic, were also the doctors for the people of their time. In fact, it is probable that they really could use herbs to cure certain diseases.

There are two instances related in the Book of Acts pertaining to pseudo-healers. The first is in chapter 8, verses 4-24. After the death of Stephen, the deacon Philip went to Samaria, where he obtained many cures and cast out demons. This was viewed as a threat to a local magician called Simon, who wanted to have the same power. Philip's cures drew the attention of the people, who then believed the Gospel as preached by Philip and were baptized. Simon (generally known as Simon Magus or Simon the magician) tried to persuade the apostles to sell him their power. Acts clearly indicates that the healing power the apostles and disciples received from God is not for sale.

The second account of a pseudo-healer is in chapter 13, verses 4-12. Paul (whose Hebrew name was Saul) went to the island of Cyprus with Barnabas and John Mark. There they visited the synagogues, preaching the Gospel. Acts tells us about a Jewish magician, or false prophet, named Bar-Jesus. His given name was Elymas, to which the people attached "Magus," meaning "the magician." The response of Paul to this opposition is reminiscent of the contest between Moses and the Egyptian priests.

Many Christian missionaries can attest that similar scenes take place in developing countries today, where the local magicians try to hold their ground against the Gospel. On a superficial level some "healers" can bring about the appearance of cures, but the true, deep substantial cure or healing can only come from God.

Healing is not a technique to be learned, but a way of life to be lived. But if baptized persons can pray over others, anoint with oil, and obtain healing through their prayers or anointing, what is that? Many early Christians, many holy persons, down through the centuries have done so. This kind of prayer and anointing is not a sacrament but a sacramental, something like a sacrament, but which obtains its power from the prayer of the Church, connected with but not fully a part of the sacraments. In the Mass God our Creator Father is present; Jesus His Son our Redeemer is present and gives Himself as resurrected, glorified God-man; and the Holy Spirit, Infinite Love, is present, with His Gifts.

All sacraments, all blessings, all blessed objects, all Christian prayer, receive power to do good from the Creator Father, the Redeemer Son, and the Sanctifier Holy Spirit, working in and through the Church.

His compassion toward all who suffer goes
so far that he identifies himself with them: "I

was sick and you visited me" (Mt 25:36) (CCC 1503).

Often Jesus asks the sick to believe (cf. Mk 5:34, 36; 9:23). He makes use of signs to heal: spittle and the laying on of hands (cf. Mk 7:32-36; 8:22-25); mud and washing (Jn 9:6-7). The sick try to touch him, "for power came forth from him and healed them all" (Lk 6:19; cf. Mt 1:41; 3:10; 6:56). And so in the sacraments Christ continues to touch us in order to heal us (CCC 1504).

Moved by so much suffering Christ not only allows himself to be touched by the sick, but he makes their miseries his own: "He took our infirmities and bore our diseases" (Mt 8:17; cf. Is 53:4) (CCC 1505).

His preferential love for the sick has not ceased through the centuries to draw the very special attention of Christians toward all those who suffer in body and soul. It is the source of tireless efforts to comfort them (CCC 1503).

Father Larry Gesy

A sign of God's will: He leads you where you do not intend to go

sign that God is working in your life is that He will lead you where you do not intend to go. Over the years most people testify that God works in strange and marvelous ways when we surrender what we want and give our lives over to God. My story is a testimony of and a witness to how God has transformed me and used me as a piece of clay that He has molded to serve Him.

I was born in Storm Lake, Iowa, on March 29, 1949. My parents were Joseph and Alvina Gesy, and I am the eldest of seven children. My parents were farmers. Farming had always been in the history of our family. My mother's family in Germany owns, lives on, and farms the same land today as they have done since the 1500s. Therefore I hardly need mention that my parents expected me as the eldest to inherit the farm and to continue the family tradition. I always loved the farm life, especially my dogs and cats. Then, in third grade, I heard a call to something other than what my parents wanted me to do.

The Sisters of St. Francis of Assisi from Clinton, Iowa, taught in our Catholic school, Our Lady of Good Counsel, in Fonda, Iowa. I loved my third grade teacher, Sister Victoria, who was so kind and loving and reminded my of my grandmother, Bertha Gesy. Sister Victoria constantly encouraged me to become a priest. Then one day a priest from a minor seminary visiting our classroom asked if any of us wanted to be priests or sisters. Of course all raised their hands. When I returned home from school that day and announced to my family that I was going to become a priest my parents just smiled and made the good Catholic response: "That's nice." I never changed my mind.

My goal of the priesthood became my daily living and breathing dream and was fostered by the excellent sisters, pastors, and associate pastors who inspired me by their lives. I was an average student who loved school and hated math! Consequently I never did well with the Iowa Basic Skills Tests and did about as poorly on my college entrance exam. Math would always pull down my scores. When I met with our associate pastor to review my scores, Father informed me that I would never make it through college because I didn't have the intelligence to succeed, a polite let-down. That was all that I needed to want to succeed even more.

In March, 1966, my family moved to Cresco, Iowa, where my parents had purchased a two-hundred-forty-acre farm. I graduated from Notre Dame High School in June, 1967, and that September entered the seminary at Loras College in Dubuque, Iowa, for the Archdiocese of Dubuque. Until that time, no one in our family had gone to college. No one in our family had ever become a priest or religious, and the farming roots ran deep. My goal of the priesthood was as clear as ever in my mind.

In college I was not outstanding, yet I graduated as an above-average student with a bachelor's degree in English and a minor in philosophy and education. I always had a nagging question about the Scripture passage from the Gospel of John, "It was not you who chose me, but I who chose you" (Jn 15:16). Did God want me as much as I wanted Him?

The major seminary, St. Bernard in Dubuque, had closed the year before my graduation from Loras College, so I was assigned by Archbishop Byrne to St. Mary Seminary and University in Baltimore for the last four years of my theological education for the priesthood. Consequently I found myself on the East Coast. I always had a sense that I was called to ministry outside of my homeland, and here I was in Baltimore. God's Divine Providence was always working in my life. Could this also be a part of His plan?

On July 14, 1972, while I was working in the seminary library, I suddenly developed severe chest pain, nausea, and pains down my left arm. I attempted to reach my room on the second floor of the huge seminary building. I made it to the second floor bathroom where I began to vomit and perspire profusely. The pain was so intense that I could hardly bear it. A friend who lived on the same floor happened to come into the bathroom at this time and found me in a serious condition. Roger took me to my room and asked me if he should call a doctor. I told him that I was all right.

In the midst of the intense pain, as I was biting the pillow on my bed, I asked him to drive me to the hospital immediately. I could not wait for an ambulance. I was rushed to the hospital and immediately taken to the emergency room.

There I was greeted by Father Daily and Sister Barbara, who asked me to receive the Last Rites of the church. I was astounded and informed them that I wasn't that sick, that my condition was not serious enough for the Last Rites. Sister Barbara only smiled as Father Daily anointed me. Five hours later I was diagnosed as having had a posterior lateral myocardial infarction, a "heart attack" that was considered very serious, especially at the age of twenty-three. Most people who have such attacks at that age never survive. I had made it to the emergency room. I woke up many hours later in the intensive care unit of St. Joseph Hospital in Towson, Maryland, operated by the Sisters of St. Francis from Glen Riddle, Pennsylvania. There were those good Franciscan sisters again.

Of course, I was wondering, at only twenty-three years old, how this heart attack would affect my life. At this point I was so close to my goal, yet so close to death. Was I going to live? Would I be handicapped? Could I pursue my education to the priesthood? How did this fit into God's Divine Providence?

My condition worsened and my parents and sister Linda were called from Iowa to the hospital in Baltimore. It was probable I wouldn't live. I was in critical condition at the time and that continued. After four days, my parents returned to Iowa, and my sister stayed as I struggled to survive.

During this time of intense pain, I kept asking God the meaning of this tragedy in my life. I fought my heart attack to such an extent that the nurses would beg me to calm down. For some reason I did not grasp the serious danger that I was in. After a few days in coronary care, a priest came to see me. Father Jack Collopy was visiting with his mother in St. Joseph's Hospital at the time. She informed him that a seminarian who was in the coronary care unit was having serious problems.

Since Father Jack was having his own vocation crisis at the time, he had tried to avoid his mother's plea that he visit me and pray for my healing. He certainly didn't need to be confronted with someone my age dying in the coronary care unit. Reluctantly he came to the unit where the nurses told him that the doctors did not expect me to live anyway, so he could do whatever he wanted. I was throwing blood clots from my lungs into my brain. Any one of them should have killed me, yet I was still alive. "Well," Father Jack said, "What have I to lose?"

I will never forget Father Jack's visit, his compassion, his prayer for healing. When he left me I knew that something extraordinary had happened. God had touched me through this very fragile and broken vessel, His priest, Father Jack. I would be changed. I had received healing. Father Jack, too, had been touched. From that moment his life was different and changed. He decided to continue in the priesthood.

I remember that the pain and the fear did not disappear, nor the doubt and the despair. Nights were a literal hell. I lay in my bed looking at the crucifix on the wall of my hospital room and asking God where He was. I remember one night, when I had reached the bottom of the pit, looking at the crucifix and asking God to make something positive happen from this heart attack. I told Him that I did not understand what was happening nor the reason but I knew that He had a reason. He had never abandoned me before.

"Please, God," I said, "I surrender my will to yours knowing that your Divine Providence will help me to face the future." From that moment, I was spiritually ready to allow God to do his work in me. Father Jack's blessing had been the beginning of my healing. Medicine, doctors, and nurses were doing their best. Now faith had to bring the work to completion.

Seventeen days later I was released from the coronary-care unit to a private room. However, my condition did not improve. I developed pleurisy, a very painful lung condition that often results from long bed rest. The pleurisy continued until I had been hospitalized for four weeks. My condition was not improving and I felt that I was being left to die. My parents insisted that I be transferred to Johns Hopkins Hospital in Baltimore, one of the best hospitals in the world. My doctor there, Nicholas Fortuin, was a nationally-acclaimed cardiovascular specialist. Immediately, under his care, my condition improved. Two weeks later I was released from the hospital.

The rector of the seminary insisted that I return home to Iowa for what was expected to be a lengthy period of recuperation. I refused, and finally we all agreed that I should stay at the seminary, which was my home. The summer gave me time to improve my health before a heart catherization scheduled for six months later. At that time, medical practice prescribed a long period of guarded rest before a heart catherization could be done to determine the cause and the extent of the damage after a heart attack. So, once school started, I was permitted to attend classes on a closed-circuit phone system between my room and the seminary classroom.

After the catherization at John Hopkins, I was informed that my heart was in very good condition. The scar tissue proved that I had had a heart attack, but the doctors could not explain, could give no medical reason, for such an extraordinary recovery with no side effects or damage to my heart. I walked out of the hospital after the heart catherization scratching my head and asking God what had happened. Even now I cannot grasp completely the scope of what had happened. To this day I have no restrictions or limitations.

The sense that I was called to ministry outside of my homeland persisted, so I decided to transfer to the Archdiocese of Baltimore, if I would be accepted. Archbishop Borders, the ordinary of the Archdiocese of Baltimore, accepted me. Was this still another part of God's providential plan?

I continued my studies and was ordained a deacon for the Archdiocese of Baltimore on October 12, 1974, by Cardinal Shehan at All Saints Church in Baltimore. A year later, I was ordained to the priesthood on October 11, 1975, at my home parish of Saint Joseph in Cresco, Iowa, by Bishop Watters, who had been the auxiliary bishop in Dubuque when I was in college at Loras. In 1975 he was the Ordinary of Winona, Minnesota, but he came to my home parish for my ordination to the priesthood, in place of the auxiliary bishop who was to ordain me, who had had a heart attack three weeks before my scheduled ordination.

My first assignment was to St. Lawrence Church in Baltimore, Maryland.

As a newly ordained priest, I was a zealous disciple for the

Church. One day while I was celebrating a baptism an individual approached me to encourage me to take a seminar that would enhance my communication skills as well as my self-image. The training was EST (Erhart Seminar Training) which was attracting a large number of professionals, clergy, and religious. During the training, I became entrenched in the belief system of Werner Erhardt. Although many persons tried to tell me that EST was a destructive movement, I did not want to believe it. How could a Catholic priest become attracted to a destructive movement?

It required much persuasion from many concerned friends to bring me to see the errors in my new beliefs and to drop the practice of the EST philosophy. I found it hard to believe that I could have been so vulnerable and so stupid as to follow such an anti-Christian practice.

Shortly after I was ordained, I was asked to anoint and pray over a boy who had been an "A" student in the fourth grade from my first parish, St. Lawrence. At Johns Hopkins Hospital, with the prayer group from the parish, I found the boy totally out of control with some kind of rare brain seizure. He could not read or concentrate for a moment. The doctors had given up all hope of recovery. In a few days he would be committed to a state institution. The prayer group and I prayed over the boy and I anointed him. Before leaving, I gave the boy a copy of the New Testament.

A few days later, the boy's mother informed me that her son had shown dramatic improvement after we left. He had picked up the Bible and had begun reading about the healings of Jesus. He hadn't been able to read for weeks because of the affliction. In a few days the boy was sent home, off all medication. The doctors were as baffled as I. I never forgot the experience, but a long period of time had to elapse before I would begin to plumb the depths of its meaning for myself and for others.

Shortly after I left my first assignment at St. Lawrence, I

was assigned as an associate pastor to St. Anthony parish in Baltimore, Maryland. By this time I had become acquainted with a woman named Doris Quelet, who was working with destructive religious movements. Doris worked with me to help me become deprogrammed from my EST belief system. During the early '80s this was called deprogramming, although today we call it exit counseling. The year that I left the movement was 1980. Doris got me on the right track and I began to work with her to help families and victims of destructive religious movements.

The grace of God had led me to realize that anyone can be duped by a movement that we now call a destructive cult. Perhaps my own limited experience in EST had given me some very deep insights into the workings of destructive religious movements. Insight into my own vulnerability and stupidity in embracing a faddish belief system brought me to study to become an expert in the area of destructive religious movements.

In this instance God had used my involvement with a false belief system, which could have been extremely destructive to me as a man and as a priest, and turned it into a means of service, just as He had first used my heart attack. His Divine Providence helped me again to use a personal experience for the good of others. I could not have foreseen that God would use my experience to liberate many persons over the years from their slavery.

Exit counseling reminds me of one of the readings that I selected for my ordination, the passage from the Gospel of Luke:

> The Spirit of the Lord is upon me,
> because he has anointed me
>   to bring glad tidings to the poor.
> He has sent me to proclaim liberty to captives
>   and recovery of sight to the blind,
>   to let the oppressed go free,

and to proclaim a year acceptable to the
Lord (Lk 4:18-19).

Shortly after I became involved in the work of exit counseling, I was asked by Father LeBar, cult consultant for the Archdiocese of New York and author of *Cults, Sects, and the New Age* (Our Sunday Visitor, 1989), to be a part of a newly-formed committee made up of priest experts in the United States who would report to Cardinal Francis Arinze, the Secretary for Non-Christian Religions at the Vatican.

The editors of Our Sunday Visitor Publishing Division wanted to produce another book on the subject of destructive religious movements, but with a different approach. So, after competing my second master's degree, this time in religious education from Marywood College in Scranton, Pennsylvania, I complied with that request in May, 1993. I asked specialists on specific aspects of cults to write the chapters on which they were experts. Some of them had become experts after having first suffered as victims of a cult.

As the cult consultant for the Archdiocese of Baltimore, with Doris Quelet, who is my associate, I have been used by God in very powerful ways. The work has lead me to incredible experiences of being before millions on television and writing a book, as well as experiencing the absolute presence of evil evidenced by those who were under the oppression and the power of the devil.

Back to the early '80s at St. Anthony: One day the prayer group at St. Anthony's asked me to celebrate a Mass after which Sister Beatrice would have blessings for healing. I had heard of Sister Beatrice Novotny, SSND (School Sisters of Notre Dame) in Baltimore, and how, although she was past retirement age, God had called her to a healing ministry. I told the prayer group that I would do it only because I was curious.

Imagine! I had had a miraculous healing and I did not want to be involved in a healing service — "All this crazy healing stuff!" — even though some of my parishioners told me that I had a gift of healing. Actually I was probably afraid of being associated with religious enthusiasts or fanatics. Even such priest healers as Fathers DiOrio and McDonough, with very active ministries, were labeled by some as "off the wall." Yet why did I run from this calling after experiencing my own miracles?

Sister Beatrice's Mass came and went. I was not that impressed, even though I knew that something extraordinary was happening at the service. Later that year I was asked to celebrate another Mass with Sister Beatrice. I agreed. Three weeks prior to the Mass and the healing service, Sister got sick and it was too late to cancel the Mass.

When I informed the congregation that evening that Sister Beatrice was sick, I told them that they should not expect any of that "crazy stuff" this evening. Yet for some reason, I told them in the next breath that Sister Beatrice was not here this evening so that God could use me and my gifts. I proceeded with the Mass not believing what I had said. After the Mass, we began the healing. Father Sears and I were in the center aisle of the church. I was watching out of the corner of my eye as people were resting in the spirit. Before I knew it the person under my hands was lying on the floor, out cold. I didn't know whether to laugh, cry, or run!

That night I saw miracles of healing such as I had never seen before. When I finished the healing service I was so elated, yet scared. God had shown me my own gift and I knew He was expecting me to return to Him what He had given me — healing. Yet, why me? I heard God whisper, "Why not?" I knew that from that moment my life would take a course quite different from what I had anticipated. I knew it was going to demand a price.

The price that I had to pay was the lack of understanding of my brother clergy. Like me, they did not understand what was happening. As I look back fourteen years later I can see why they did not feel comfortable with the healing ministry. In June, 1982,

I founded the Catholic Healing Ministry of Baltimore. This is a ministry of healing involving clergy, religious, and laity.

Shortly after Thanksgiving, on December 2, 1982, only a few months after the beginning of the healing ministry, I developed abdominal pain that led me to being hospitalized at Mercy Hospital in Baltimore. I thought the purpose of the healing ministry was to bring healing. Here I was in the hospital in excruciating pain.

Seventeen days later, after the prayers of many people, including Sister Beatrice, and the work of the doctors, I was diagnosed with a blood clot in a vein leading around my stomach into my intestine. The lack of blood flow to the intestine should have resulted in loss of a major part of the intestine, but again I walked out of the hospital healed. God does take care of His own.

This experience gave me a deeper insight into healing. I remember praying once that God would teach me something about healing. He taught me that there are many kinds of healing. Never ask God for anything unless you are ready and prepared to receive it.

I remember a meeting with Sister Beatrice when I asked her about the mysteries of how God healed His people through the use of the healing hands of others. She informed me that she did not concern herself about the why's but just tried to do His will. "Papa," she said, "takes care in His own way. It is not ours to ask, but to trust." Sister said that the many stories of healing in the New Testament that occurred two thousand years ago are just as relevant for us today. If Jesus gave the command to bring healing and reconciliation to the Church, didn't He also give the power to His disciples? We are His disciples through baptism and ordination. It made sense to me, perhaps more so than anything that I had heard before.

At that time, a little less than twenty years ago, many priests and laity in the Catholic church looked with a suspicious eye on this phenomenon called "healing." Healing was associated with the charismatic movement. Sister Beatrice helped me to distinguish the difference between the charismatic movement and the charisms of the Holy Spirit that are recorded in the writings of St. Paul in the New Testament.

My first discussion with Sister Beatrice was my last. She died six months later on October 19, 1983, at the age of eighty-eight! God had laid the foundation by giving me some tidbits of learning at the feet of one of his beloved children and disciples, Sister Beatrice. Gradually God was teaching me to use the charism to be an instrument of healing like Sister Beatrice. Sister Beatrice and I never talked about what would happen to the ministry she was given. Being in her eighties she trusted that "Papa" would take care of it — and He did! Her ministry was placed in my hands like the passing of a baton in a race. Most priests in the healing ministry will attest to similar experiences, being duped by God in a gentle way to this calling. Jeremiah gently chides God for the same thing:

> You duped me, O LORD, and I let myself be
> duped;
> you were too strong for me, and you tri-
> umphed.
> All the day I am an object of laughter;
> everyone mocks me (Jer 20:7).

God is the "Hound of Heaven." He is patient and gradually leads the horse into the stable with a bit of hay and then He very slowly closes the gate. He always gets what He wants in His time and not in ours, in His ways and not in our ways. Most priests in healing ministry will tell you that they were duped by God in the same way!

In November, 1988, my sister called me to tell me that our mother had cancer of the stomach and the esophagus. She was scheduled to have major surgery in eight days. The prognosis was not good. I knew that I had to be there to bring the sacraments to her as well as to my father and my brothers and sisters. I had to practice what I preached.

I flew to Iowa and met my sister. We went to the hospital in LaCrosse, Wisconsin, and arrived the evening before surgery. When I entered her room, my mother was so surprised to see me. I immediately asked her if a priest had been there to anoint her. She said no. She had asked four times that day but no one had arrived. I told her that I had come to anoint her and give her the Holy Eucharist before the surgery. She was immediately at peace as I administered the sacrament. So was I. It was as though years of hurt and pain in our difficult relationship were washed away with the stroke of one encounter with Christ in the sacrament of the Anointing of the Sick. The more that we are healed, the more God can use us as His wounded healers.

My mother's health improved, but in December, 1988, my mother's mother, my grandmother Kathryn, died at the age of ninety-three. Then on February 24, 1989, my father was killed in a tragic trucking accident in Virginia. During the farm crisis in the '80s my parents had lost the farm they had worked on for all their lives, and moved into town in Cresco, Iowa. My father began working for a small business that made horse trailers. He had been asked to drive the new trailers to different parts of the country. He had never been off the farm nor away from his family for sixty-five years. He died alone, a thousand miles away from home. After my father's death Mom's health diminished rapidly. She died on November 13, 1989, at the age of sixty-one.

The trauma of dealing with three deaths in one year probably would be more than one could endure without faith. One of my favorite road signs on the way to Lancaster, Pennsylvania, says, "Those who live without faith live without hope." How true!

I knew that God had made everything right before the death of my parents. With the strength of our faith and the support of family and friends, my sisters and brothers and I were able to cope with these tragic losses. The healing power of Jesus Christ in the Eucharist and the Anointing of the Sick gave us the strength we needed. I was taught again to trust in His ways. The relationship between my mother and me had been healed, yet she was not healed physically. Why? God's ways are not our ways. I have only learned to trust more. That's faith.

Ordinarily, the third kind of healing, physical healing, seems to be the primary motivator of people seeking God's powers. When you are sick you are sick! I believe that everyone in healing ministries needs to experience being seriously sick or faced with the sickness of loved ones. I do not wish this on anyone, yet it is a most valuable experience, because it truly humbles one before God to feel the helplessness of being in one or both of these situations.

As I am writing this chapter, my best priest friend and pastor of Holy Rosary Church in Baltimore is undergoing open heart surgery at Johns Hopkins for a valve replacement. Fortunately he is blessed to have the best doctors in the world for such a major surgery — his cardiologist, Dr. Nicholas Fortuin, and his surgeon, Dr. Peter Greene. Before Dr. Greene began Father Ron's surgery, I remember saying to him, "Peter, may the Lord bless your hands."

Never before had I placed such trust into anyone's hands. This is complete surrender to God using the hands of a physician to restore health to a very special person and priest to many people. Suddenly I understood what trust in medicine meant to me. Faith in God includes realizing that God wills that each of His children should use well the knowledge and skills He has given to us, so when we put ourselves in the hands of a good doctor, we are also entrusting ourselves to that doctor's Creator. Medicine does not work miracles, but the Creator of the doctors who have made great discoveries or who have developed great skill is the One who works miracles through His doctor-children.

Physical healing involves the use of the behavioral and medical sciences to restore health. Why does God want us to be well? We have work to do in this world. He also wants us to give witness by our healings so that others might believe. All the stories of healing in the Scriptures are intended to lead us to believe in, to have faith in, Jesus Christ. Sickness is the result of the sin of Adam and Eve in the garden. From the point of their fall, humankind became subject to sickness, suffering, and death. Yet as long as the world exists, suffering will exist. God does not cause it; He permits it.

In our need and desire to be made whole, God wants us to seek Him first when the worst things in the world happen to us. We place our faith in many people, daily trusting they know what they are doing and are worthy of our trust. It is a leap of faith to entrust your car to a mechanic, your home to a carpenter, etc. God uses the hands of all in their special charism and career to serve Him and the world. When a doctor is operating on a patient, he is being used by God as though the physician's hands are His.

People relate in many ways both to religious faith and to medical science. I believe it is necessary to consult doctors and to use medicine. I never tell anyone to throw away his or her medicine and stop seeing their doctors. That is not an act of faith, but of dangerous foolhardiness. I take medicine to lower cholesterol and see my doctors regularly. I strongly encourage individuals with emotional problems or any serious problem to seek the assistance of good professional help in the psychiatric field. Balance and good sense make the best sense!

The final area of healing is the freeing of oppression, obsession, and even demonic possession. What is the greatest monster or oppression in your life? Is it fear, guilt, low self-image? Some of the worst forms of oppression are passed on from generation to generation in our families. Our co-dependent behaviors can control our lives for an entire lifetime. Healing of the oppression in families and preventing the spread of that oppression into the world needs major attention. To test the truth of that statement, keep that in mind while you read the newspaper and watch television.

In May, 1990, I made a pilgrimage to Medjugorje. The experiences of pilgrims to Medjugorje, although not confirmed by the Church, have brought healing to the lives of many people. Any movement is known by its fruits. I was overwhelmed by the faith and the trust of the pilgrims. Every kind of healing was taking place. As a priest in a healing ministry, I must say that it confirmed my faith to see such love of the Church and the sacraments, especially the Eucharistic Presence. God's healing power appeared to be seeping out of the pores of the village.

My Medjugorje experience brought letting go of a lot of oppression, especially fear and doubt, that had lingered in my life for years. I was always afraid of being hurt by the reactions of others. This is probably true for most of us. I prayed for the gifts of the Holy Spirit, especially boldness and trust, in addition to the healing of any generational problems in my family. My grandmother and both of my parents were on my mind constantly, that they would be at peace in heaven. My prayers were answered in ways unimaginable. I still reap the fruits of this experience.

The greatest gift was seeing the love that Father Joso has for the Eucharist and how that love empowers him to make himself an instrument of healing. I experienced the love of Mary, the spinning of the sun, and the singing of the birds at night. The beauty of it all pointed to Jesus Christ in the mystery of the Eucharist and in the visible community of the Church and its believers. Many who have visited Medjugorie have attempted to recreate this same faith in our parishes, our families, and in the various forms of spiritual renewal such as retreats and Marian Conferences that have come about in recent years.

The great gift of boldness has given me courage to face some serious evil that I and the healing team have seen in our ministry. The devil does exist and he occasionally raises his ugly head. The first time that I saw a manifestation of a spirit in an oppressed person, it scared the hell back into me. Please excuse the use of the word but I do mean it. But allow me to give a word of caution. Beware of any deliverance ministry that sees the devil under every rock and around every corner. I have seen much damage to personalities and have heard of many disastrous personal experiences coming from such movements. It is even more serious for anyone in healing ministry to tell an individual that he or she is not made well or healed because of his or her lack of faith!

(You can read more about oppression, obsession, and demonic possession in my book *Today's Destructive Cults and Movements* published by Our Sunday Visitor, 1993.)

As a priest, I always wanted to become a pastor of a parish. God used a route which took me into the ministry of healing and cult awareness. This seems to be what He wanted from me. In His will is my peace, and I live by this statement of faith. I did not choose the way that He has led, but it is an exciting journey of faith even with its many rocky paths.

On July 1, 1994, I became the interim pastor of a small parish called St. Joseph's in Taneytown, Maryland. I was sent to prepare the way for the new pastor who would arrive in February, 1995. I felt as if I were living *The Diary of a Country Priest*. I loved the people, and the few months of that ministry were such a blessing. It prepared me for the next stage of the journey, which was to become an actual pastor.

On February 24, 1995, I was made the pastor of St. Francis of Assisi in Brunswick, and St. Mary in Petersville, Maryland. These two parishes, located near Harpers Ferry, West Virginia, are full of history. Both parishes need a great deal of healing and restoring of hope. The parishioners are pure gold. When I arrived I asked them to assist in the building up of the spiritual community by praying for the gifts of the Holy Spirit. Currently we are working to build ministries and organizations. A pastor does not have buildings, but rather the living stones that make up the spiritual house (see 1 Pt 2:5), the people of God.

God will build on the foundation of faith. I am so happy that God called me and allows me to be a pastor, a healer, an administrator, a teacher, and primarily a priest.

In October, 1995, I took part in a seminar held in San Giovanni Rotundo, the former home of Padre Pio. Five hundred persons from every country in the world gathered to pray and learn about evangelization and healing. Fifteen were from the United States. What is the next phase of the journey?

As I continue my pastorate, the healing ministry, and the cult ministry, I am conscious even more of the Eucharist as the source and center of all healing. When I was writing my first book on destructive cults in 1992 and 1993, I was involved in the Baltimore Marian Conferences. Someone encouraged me to ask Mother Teresa of Calcutta to write the foreword to my book. I did, but I knew the demands placed on this modern saint.

Mother Teresa opened a new convent in Baltimore at the same time that I was writing the book. I was invited to be at the Mass dedicating the Mission of Charity and the Chapel for the sisters. Two days before this event I dreamed that Mother Teresa came to see me at Our Lady of Victory rectory where I was the associate pastor. I was so overwhelmed as she walked into my room that I knelt down to kiss her hand. The most profound impact of the dream was about the Eucharist. I was moved by the thought of meeting a living saint, yet how casual we can become about receiving the Eucharist. As I remember the dream, it ended with Mother giving me the foreword for my book.

I didn't understand the meaning of the dream until I saw Mother Teresa in person at St. Wenceslaus in Baltimore at the dedication Mass celebrated by (now) Cardinal William Keeler, the Archbishop of Baltimore. Mother Teresa was in the front pew with her sisters. I was in the sanctuary observing her during the Mass. Her love of Christ in the Eucharist was deeply moving, reflective of her saintliness. When she knelt on the kneeler next to me after the Mass for the dedication of the chapel I thought that a dream of my life had been fulfilled. I even kissed her hand as I had in my dream. I floated home to find an airmail letter from India. It was the foreword to the book from Mother Teresa, hand-written.

I must quote a passage from that foreword by Mother Teresa. It compresses a lifetime of reflection. Even if you don't read all of my book on destructive religious movements, and I hope that you do, you must read this foreword.

> Jesus not only came to preach Good News to the poor. He became the Poor One — the hungry one, the homeless one. And He said: "What you do to the least of My brothers, that you do to Me." Jesus in the least of our brothers is not only hungry for bread but He is also hungry for love. This hunger for love is in fact hunger for God, for God is Love. The nakedness in today's world is not only for clothes. The real nakedness in our world today is the need for our human dignity. The greatest poverty today is the poverty of not knowing who we are — of not knowing that we are the Children of God — that we have a Father in heaven Who cares for us tenderly. The poorest of the poor today are those who do not know they are created for greater things — to love and to be loved and to share the joy of loving with one another. They seek to nourish their souls on the falsehood found in destructive religious movements.

> If we really center our lives on Jesus, if we really understand the Eucharist and nourish our souls with the Bread of Life and the word of God, we would not only be able to recognize the likeness of God in ourselves and oth-

ers but we would also be able to restore it to those who seem to have lost it. My prayer is that all who read this book may realize that: Jesus is the Truth to tell; the Word to speak; the Way to walk; the Love to share; and the Life to live — the fullness of life which Jesus Himself came to give us.

— Mother Teresa

I hope that I have given you something to change your life and to help you to become more like Christ in your daily encounters. I leave you with this message: The ultimate healing is death! That's true. In this world, complete dying to self means complete surrender and trust such as we see in the life of Mother Teresa. To me Mother Teresa is a perfect example of how each of us can completely die to self and surrender completely to God. Being in her presence makes one aware that there is a lot of dying to self still to be done. However, Mother Teresa in her humility will admit that she has much to do in her own work of sanctification! All of us are called to be saints. The Eucharist, this frail giant will tell you, is her dynamo, the source of her power. The Eucharist is the key to all healing. More and more of my ministry of healing is centered around the Real Eucharistic Presence on the altar and in Eucharistic adoration and benediction. Many parishes are seeing the impact of devotion to the Eucharist.

Finally, yes, the greatest healing is death in the physical sense. By then hopefully we will have learned the lesson of complete surrender and trust. St. Paul says: "For I am convinced that neither death, nor life, nor angels, nor principalities, nor present things, nor future things, nor powers, nor height, nor depth, nor any other creature will be able to separate us from the love of God in Christ Jesus our Lord" (Rom 8:38-39).

I believe that the most difficult thing about writing this book is that there always seems to be something new happening, some new event or experience, which is another story. Life is like an onion with many layers. We can expect the good with the bad. In the course of a lifetime everyone will experience a variety of levels of joy and sorrow. Our faith and trust in God will determine whether we will become bitter individuals who turn our backs on God believing that He is the cause of it all or individuals who will grow spiritually seeing Him as the Divine Healer. Today I have two masters' degrees, am a pastor of two churches, have written two books, founded and directed a healing and cult ministry, all thanks to God.

Oh, yes, I almost forgot. Never say never.

Anna L. Marshall

Introduction to St. Anne

cannot recall the first time I was taken by my parents to visit the Shrine of St. Anne at St. Jean Baptiste Church on Lexington Avenue, New York. What I can recall very vividly is that at least several times a year, and most certainly whenever one or another family member or friend had some special need, my parents and I would make a mini-pilgrimage ("mini" because we lived only about an hour away) to St. Anne's Shrine as part of our "prayer package."

St. Anne was an integral part of our family, and I heard many times how that had come about. My maternal grandparents, George and Anna Brennan Zincke, lived in Brooklyn with their two young boys and were expecting another child. At baptism, my grandmother had been named for St. Anne. When she was eight months pregnant, she eagerly traveled from Brooklyn to Manhattan to visit the Church of St. Jean Baptiste while the relic of St. Anne was there. I do not know the date of her visit to St. Jean Baptiste, but her daughter, Anna, was born on June 12, 1892.

When Father Larry Gesy told me about Susan Bradford's cure at St. Anne de Beaupré (detailed in the next chapter) and said that the account of that cure would be included in this book, I recalled the small pamphlet that had come down to me in the box of prayer books and rosaries that had belonged to my grandmother. It seemed appropriate to include the account of those events to show how cures and healings today are present counterparts of events which have taken place in every century of our history as the People of God.

What follows is an abridgement of the pamphlet "The Good St. Anne, Mother of the Blessed Virgin Mary and Her Shrine in the Church of Saint Jean Baptiste, New York City," by Right Reverend Bernard O'Reilly D.D. of Laval, P.Q., printed by the Blessed Sacrament Fathers, 1919. It is faithful to the facts and almost exclusively in Monsignor O'Reilly's own words, omitting only some of the florid Victorian language which would seem strange to us who live a hundred years later.

— Anna L. Marshall

Cures Said to be Wrought in New York, in May 1892, on the Occasion of the Passage Through that City of a Relic of St. Anne, the Mother of the Blessed Virgin Mary.

We are writing these lines on the 21st of May, 1892, after the departure from New York of Right Reverend Monsignor J. C. Marquis.

The three weeks which have elapsed since Sunday the first May (1892) have been marked by an extraordinary manifestation of Catholic faith and piety." Monsignor J. C. Marquis, Protonotary Apostolic, arrived at the rectory of St. Jean Baptiste (St. Jean Baptiste is French for St. John the Baptist. The Church is located at the corner of Lexington Avenue and 76th Street, New York City, staffed by French-speaking priests to serve the French and French-Canadian people living in and around New York) unheralded and unexpected, bearing from Rome a relic of St. Anne, the mother of the Blessed Virgin Mary, sent by Pope Leo XIII to the Shrine of Sainte Anne de Beaupré, near Quebec. As soon as the Reverend Frederick Tetreau and his assistants discovered that Monsignor Marquis was the bearer of a relic of St. Anne, a fragment of the wrist bone some two or three inches in length, they requested that Monsignor Marquis allow it to be exposed to the veneration of the parishioners during the Vesper service that evening, as he was to start for Quebec the next day. The Reliquary was taken to the church.

In the interval between Mass and Vespers it became widely known that the faithful would have an opportunity to venerate the relic at the evening service. The church was densely crowded with the sick and suffering and others who had come to beseech the Good St. Anne, as she is fondly called in France and in Canada, to obtain of God the cures they desired.

One alleged cure that evening caught the attention of the crowd. What follows is the account of eyewitnesses, as they described the occurrence.

A young man, an epileptic of many years' standing, came to the railing, accompanied by his father. He fell into fearful convulsions as he approached the relic. It took the utmost strength of several men to hold down this unfortunate. But no sooner did the priest touch the poor sufferer's person with the Reliquary than the convulsions ceased. We do not know whether or not this young man was permanently relieved from his malady. His family are well known.

The sudden cessation of the epileptic spasms, and the awe which fell upon all present, as if Christ once more was visibly visiting His people, struck the great city like a mighty electric shock. The eager crowds of visitors who kept thronging to the church, long after the usual Vesper hours, were a forewarning of what was in preparation for the morrow. All through that day and next, and the next again, and far into the night the living stream of needy petitioners for health of body and soul filled the usually quiet and out-of-the-way little church.

Monsignor Marquis, after this first consoling experience of Sunday the first of May, was persuaded to remain in New York a few days longer. He had obtained the authorization of his superiors. So the relic was exposed throughout the entire week. The devotion of the people grew with each successive day.

The writer of these pages more than once happened to come among the crowd outside in the street when they had just been deeply moved at the sight of some sufferer who had been helped into the church a cripple, or partly blind, or bowed down by some severe infirmity, then who suddenly came out of the church exclaiming that he was cured. This emotion was shared by the police officers at the door. Similar scenes of enthusiastic faith and gratitude were enacted in the church itself.

The first and second weeks of May ended without satisfying the ardent piety of the people. It is calculated that during these weeks from two-hundred-thousand to three-hundred-thousand persons venerated the relic of St. Anne. Many returned again and again.

The third week of May came and ended. Yet, like the multitudes who once followed Our Lord into the solitudes beyond the Lake of Gennesareth, these could not be sent away disappointed. Instead of decreasing, the multitudes who daily came steadily increased. . . . From the New England and the Middle States — from Boston, from Philadelphia, Scranton, Pittsburgh, and Baltimore . . . the movement had already acquired proportions and a momentum which baffled all calculation and prevision.

From the South and Far West, from Louisiana and Salt Lake, from Iowa, Nebraska, Wisconsin, and Minnesota letters came earnestly beseeching Monsignor Marquis to delay still another week his departure for Canada. It was impossible. The twentieth of May had to be fixed and announced as the last day for the relic's stay with us.

This last week must ever remain memorable in the religious annals of this city. There was no means of keeping an accurate account of the numbers and names of those who were daily said to be cured. Throughout these three weeks, everything had been absolutely unexpected and unforeseen. No one was appointed to keep a list of these reported miraculous happenings. No one could register the names, residence, and the specific nature of the disease, together with the witness to the chronic condition of the sufferer, as well as to the sudden recovery. Besides, the priests attached to the church were overwhelmed and exhausted, and, at first at least, few, if any, had a notion that they might need such assistance.

So all through these eventful weeks, with a few exceptions, the persons who were said to have been healed through God's power came, unknown to the multitude around them, and left, without leaving behind them any further record. Several pairs of crutches remained near the sanctuary to attest a wonderful and instant cure. Quite a number of "spectacles" were left to be hung up around the altar by persons relieved of their blindness. Other persons thanked God for the sudden end of torturing pain, or the disappearance of what threatened to be a fatal tumor, or a seemingly incurable deafness, or rheumatism which had produced deformities and prevented them from working, and so on.

Monsignor O'Reilly's account of the last week and final day of the visit to New York of the relic of St. Anne in May of 1892 is particularly moving:

. . . During the last week, made up as it was of one or two days of sunshine, breaking the monotony of continuous rain and storm, the crowds of pilgrims showed no signs of diminishing in numbers and fervor. Thursday, the 19th of May, was very stormy, the rain falling without intermission and the fierce easterly wind lashing the streets and sidewalks and rendering it difficult for the strongest arm to hold up an umbrella. Still, from five o'clock in the morning until ten at night, the street before the church, from Third to Lexington Avenues, continued to be filled with a throng of pilgrims. . . . The sidewalk above and below the church was densely packed by all who had strength enough to stand and wait. On the opposite side of the street stood hundreds apparently expecting their turn. . . . What a sight it was to look down from the sanctuary railing on the slowly advancing throng of men and women, whose features were lit up with an expression of faith and hope and ardent supplication!

. . . The relic was to be taken away at noon (Friday, June 20th) — so it had been daily announced during the last week. And in addition to the throng which were sure to come in from New York and the adjacent cities, hundreds were coming from distant parts of the country. All through the morning hours the pilgrims crowded the street and flowed in one continuous stream through the church, till the moment for Monsignor Marquis' departure was near at hand. At length four o'clock struck. . . . From every part of the edifice people endeavored to reach the priest, stretching out their arms, and crying out. . . .

. . . One of our informants, an old and most respectable citizen of New York, and a convert to the Catholic Church, was deeply interested from almost the very beginning in these wonderful daily scenes in the Church of St. Jean Baptiste. Several hours were daily spent by this person — one day nine hours, and six another were passed inside the sanctuary of St. Jean Baptiste, contemplating the wonderful and edifying spectacle.

The priests, who succeeded each other all this time in presenting the Reliquary to the lips of the pilgrims, had their eyes continually filled with tears, so moving was the sight of these faces lit up with hope and love. It was a terrible strain on the priest . . . to maintain his position, and to economize every moment of time while satisfying every person there, and keeping the dense throng moving regularly forward. . . . "Be generous!" good Father Tetreau would say to all, urging them not to be selfish in detaining the Reliquary too long, and to hasten to pass out as quickly as they could, when they had had their chance.

One who looked down upon that crowd of the suffering and the poor could not imagine what other kind of generosity they were asked to practice than not taking up the time of others, or not standing in the way of the sick and the crippled behind and around them.

Monsignor O'Reilly relates that the events of those three weeks in May moved Pope Leo XIII to send a second relic of St. Anne, this time to New York. Monsignor Marquis delivered it on July 15, 1892, the first day of a novena which would end on the Feast Day of St. Anne, July 26:

During that novena two extraordinary cures took place which Monsignor O'Reilly announced. His written account is dated August 7, 1892: Yesterday a man from Albany, with an incurable tumor in his throat, was, in an instant, on touching the relic, relieved from every trace of the tumor. And, not long afterwards, a child horribly deformed by spine disease was carried to the shrine, and on kissing the relic was cured of the disease and deformity.

What was and is so special about Beaupré?

Devotion to the Holy Family of Nazareth, to the parents of the Blessed Virgin Mary, and to the saints related to her strengthens the faith of Christians and fosters their piety towards Jesus.

This was the inspiration which moved the apostle of Canada, Francis de Laval-Montmorency, first bishop of Quebec, to consecrate his clergy and his people to the Holy Family. He authorized the printing of a narrative of several miraculous cures which had taken place in the church or chapel built in honor of St. Anne. It was written by Reverend Thomas Morel and was limited to the cures obtained through the intercession of St. Anne "during the six years he had lived at Beaupré, as missionary, from 1661 to 1667."

The first recorded miraculous cure was that of Louis Guimont. The governor of the colony had laid the cornerstone of the first church in March, 1658, but progress with building was slow because of the small number of settlers in the neighborhood, their poverty, and the war with the Iroquois. In 1661, Louis Guimont, crippled with rheumatic pains, "was moved to place with his own hands a few stones in the slowly rising walls. . . . He was cured on the spot. . . . Other wonderful cures followed year after year."

In 1665, while Father Morel was still pastor of Beaupré, the Venerable Marie of the Incarnation, foundress of the Ursuline Sisters of Quebec, wrote to a relative in France: "Some twenty miles from this . . . is a church of St. Anne, in which Our Lord works great wonders for the sake of that holy mother of the Most Blessed Virgin Mary. There one sees the paralytics walking, the blind recovering their eyesight, and the sick of every kind restored to health."

In 1890 the new Basilica of St. Anne had been completed at Beaupré. The relic sent by Pope Leo XIII was delivered in 1892 by Monsignor Marquis to the Cardinal-Archbishop of Quebec at the Shrine on July 26, Feast of St. Anne.

And what about New York?

Later a much larger stone church of St. Jean Baptiste was built, with a magnificent altar, where the Blessed Sacrament Fathers spend hours of prayer throughout the day before Jesus in the Holy Eucharist exposed in a beautiful monstrance. They adore and thank God for those who forget to adore and thank Him as well as for themselves and for all the Church. They pray for God's mercy and forgiveness for our sins and the sins of the world, and they ask that God's blessings be poured out on us all.

Beneath that upper church honoring Jesus our Savior and Healer, in the lower church, is the Shrine of St. Anne, containing the relic which Monsignor Marquis brought to the Church of St. Jean Baptiste on July 15, 1892. The crutches and other testimonials of cures granted through St. Anne's intercession for us are increased year by year until now.

We can visit one of the shrines of St. Anne at Apt in France, at Beaupré, in the Province of Quebec, at the Church of St. Jean Baptiste on Lexington Avenue at 76th Street in New York City, or we can ask her to pray with us for some special need in our own parish church or in the privacy of our home, but what is of primary importance is that each of us needs to recognize that by baptism we have been incorporated into Christ. Big words? The most important words in each of our lives. It means that we are part of the Mystical Body of Christ. Recall Jesus' words from the cross:

"When Jesus saw his mother and the disciple there whom he loved, he said to his mother, 'Woman, behold, your son.' Then he said to the disciple, 'Behold, your mother.' And from that hour the disciple took her into his home" (Jn 19:26-27).

Photo courtesy of Susan Bradford

Statue of St. Anne holding her infant daughter Mary.

A long tradition in the Church sees in those words Jesus entrusting to his mother, Mary, the apostles, and so the whole young Church and a call to us to "take her into our homes." It is no great step from Jesus and Mary to her mother, His grandmother, Anne. The one who brought up Mary, certainly part of Jesus' family, should be part of ours. We may say that we know almost nothing about her, but those very few facts should be enough.

Thy will be done

On January 2, 1977, my life as I had known it ended and my spiritual journey began. My husband, Dick, our two children, Kelly, nine, and Craig, seven, and I were visiting our longtime family friends Bill and Nancy and their three daughters for the weekend. They lived on a farm in northern Maryland. Bill was planning to build a log cabin and needed some help cutting and transporting the logs to the building site. Dick had agreed to help him while we were visiting. We arrived Friday evening, December 31, 1976, to celebrate the New Year together. Saturday was uneventful. Dick and Bill spent the day cutting the logs.

We planned to attend Mass early on Sunday, in order to give Bill and Dick more time to work. It was a frigid January morning as we left Bill and Nancy's to attend Mass. I remember praying for everyone's safety during Mass because I had a strange intuition that something was going to go very wrong. I asked God that whatever was going to happen, please don't allow anyone to suffer the loss of life.

When we arrived back at the house, the kids went out to play. Bill and Dick started to plan how they were going to move the logs up the steep hill which the cabin would overlook. Nancy and I were in the house keeping warm over hot tea. I didn't say anything about the intuition I had during Mass.

It wasn't long before Bill called Nancy and me out to the work site for our assistance. It was bitter cold out so we bundled up. I put on my new hiking boots to keep my feet warm. This simple act of changing my shoes would carry ramifications that I could not have anticipated.

When we arrived at the building site, we found that Bill had devised a pulley system to move the logs from the base of the hill up to the building location. A long piece of rope was tied to a log at the bottom of the hill. It was then threaded through a large steel pulley attached to the bumper of a stationary car, and the other end was tied to the bumper of a second car that would move. I was to signal Nancy, who was driving the car in reverse, in order to pull the logs up the hill and stop when they reached the top.

The third log was coming up the steep incline when I saw Bill and Nancy's five-year-old-daughter, Debbie, hanging onto the rope for a free ride up the hill. Knowing that at the base of the incline were boulders and below that a stream, all I could envision was that if the rope broke she would be killed. I stepped in front of the taut rope and released Debbie's grip. Carrying her, I put her down in the safety zone behind the rope.

Seconds later, before I could return to the safety zone, the hook on the pulley straightened up, releasing it from the bumper and thrusting it into my leg. The impact threw me about four feet. When I regained consciousness, I was lying on a pile of boulders in a great deal of pain and unable to move.

Bill recognized the seriousness of the situation. He immobilized my leg. It was determined there was no time to wait for an ambulance. Dick and Bill carefully placed me in the back seat of our car and Dick drove me to the hospital.

Since I was a registered nurse, I also recognized the seriousness of the situation. I knew I was going into shock, so I gave careful instructions to Nancy, who was riding with us, that I be taken to the Sinai Hospital in Baltimore (where I had received nurses' training) and to be sure I was treated by Dr. Smulyan, whom I knew and respected from my days at Sinai. The Lord was definitely looking after me that day. As it turned out Dr. Smulyan was on duty that afternoon.

As serious as my condition was, I remember lying on the examining table in the emergency room trying to convince the nurses to remove my new jeans and boots without damaging them. I can remember myself saying, "They are brand new hiking boots. Don't destroy them." Unknown to me, I would never wear those boots again. My leg had been crushed. Although I had worn the boots to keep my feet warm, I was told that they had saved my foot from amputation. God, undoubtedly, was with me that fateful afternoon. This was only the beginning of an ordeal that was to span the next fifteen-and-a-half years of my life.

For the next ten years, although I could walk (using a cane only when I absolutely needed it), I experienced chronic leg pain, multiple hospitalizations, and multiple surgeries. Unsuccessful treatments for pain relief ranged from physical therapy to ultrasound, to wearing an electric stimulator, to acupuncture and bio-feedback. I wore a heavy white stocking (called a Jobst stocking) designed to maintain my circulation and control the swelling. I also ruptured a disc in my back that made wearing a back brace necessary. But this was all tolerable.

On the morning of December 22, 1986, I woke up in a great deal of pain, my leg swollen three times its size. I was unable to walk. After retrieving a pair of crutches from the attic, Dick called my orthopedist. His first impression was that I either had incurred a stress fracture or had developed a neuroma, which is an extremely painful tumor made up of nerve endings that sit right below the surface of the skin. It proved to be neither. Several months later, and after extensive testing and consultations with numerous doctors, we were told that I was in the advanced stages of a relatively rare neurological disease called reflex sympathetic dystrophy (RSD).

More surgeries and experimental treatments followed. All were unsuccessful. The treatments included physical therapy, occupational therapy, serial casting of my foot, spinal injections of anesthesia called sympathetic blocks, a chemical sympathectomy, water therapy, and spinal catheters hooking me to a mini-computer that I wore around my waist for weeks at a time.

My condition continued to deteriorate. The pain I felt was exquisite. I developed severe asthma, carpal tunnel syndrome in both hands from using the crutches, osteoporosis, arthritis, respiratory infections, severe sinus infections, depression, and allergies or sensitivities to all of my medications.

Amputation of the leg below the knee was thought to be the final solution to pain management. However, due to my tendency to develop neuromas, I most likely would not be able to wear a prothesis. However, this was not a solution to RSD or any of its related problems. My condition would continue to deteriorate. Dr. Smulyan used to say, "If it weren't for bad luck, I wouldn't have any at all."

By August, 1992, I felt certain that I did not have long to live. My condition was deteriorating rapidly. Tests indicated liver damage, due to one of the pain medications I took. I was experiencing heart palpitations and skipped heartbeats regularly. My stamina was very poor. I had difficulty walking more that five feet at a time without stopping to rest. I just didn't feel I could fight it anymore.

As I attended Mass on the morning of August 9, 1992, I realized that my life was no longer in the hands of the doctors, but in God's hands. It was then that I surrendered my life to Jesus Christ. As I prayed the "Our Father," as I had prayed thousands of times, I suddenly understood the deep significance of the phrase "Thy will be done." I asked that whatever God's will would be that I please be given the inner peace and the strength needed to cope with whatever was coming. Since my condition was deteriorating rapidly, I felt sure it was my impending death. I asked God to take the fears and anxieties which were consuming me and carry them for me. I felt that I could no longer handle them.

Returning from Communion, I knew my prayers had been answered. I felt the peace I had been searching for. As we left church that day, I told Dick I had a compelling feeling that I had to go to the Shrine of Sainte Anne de Beaupré in Quebec City during our upcoming, and what I thought would be my last, vacation. I didn't understand why I felt the need to go, since I knew so little about the shrine, other than of its architectural beauty. We had originally planned to visit the shrine only if time permitted. Dick didn't question my feelings. St. Anne's became a definite part of our agenda.

My husband, daughter, and I left for vacation the next morning. Knowing that I would be going to St. Anne's sustained me. But I couldn't understand why I was being drawn there.

We arrived at our hotel in Springfield, Massachusetts, shortly before dinner time. It had been a long and exhausting trip, although I had slept most of the way. While at dinner, I suddenly became congested, as though I was suffering from a severe head cold. My head was filled with fluid. I couldn't imagine what was happening. I couldn't eat. Because of the intensity of the congestion, I became concerned for my already-labored breathing. I left the restaurant hoping that something there had triggered an allergic reaction. But no such luck. I was getting worse. We returned to our room. I took some medication, and after approximately two hours, my head cleared up. There were no signs of a cold. For the next two days, my congestion returned every time I went into an air-conditioned building or ate a meal. It reached a point that I was afraid to eat. I was really scared. I had never experienced anything like this before.

By the morning of August 12, the medication was no longer effective. The congestion was not going away. Dick was so concerned for my health that he suggested that we turn around and head for home. I considered it for a moment, then I told him that I had to be at St. Anne's. If I could only get there, I would be okay. I knew that I needed to be there regardless of the consequences. I wasn't sure what "okay" meant or why I had this driving force telling me to go to St. Anne's, but we continued.

Shortly after crossing the border, we stopped at an information station to exchange our currency. While there, Kelly picked up a brochure on the Shrine of Sainte Anne de Beaupré for me. In the car I read and reread it. I remember holding onto it as if it were my most prized possession. The shrine was beginning to become a reality to me. I started to feel secure. Yet I still didn't understand why!

We arrived at our hotel at 4:15 p.m. My luck was running true to form, going from bad to worse. The only available room was not accessible for people with disabilities. I was really upset by this point. I was exhausted and sick and my apprehension returned. I agreed to stay only because I was too tired to look for another place. An accessible room would become available the next morning and we would move.

I began to climb the two flights of steps to the second floor. Steps frightened me. On too many occasions I had fallen. My leg seemed to have a mind of its own. It would twist one way and I would go another. By the time I reached our room, Dick and Kelly had already made several trips carrying our luggage, including the suitcase full of my braces and medications. I just wanted to lie down and rest. A short while later, Dick suggested that we drive out to the shrine right away. My excitement was tempered with apprehension. I didn't know what to expect. I had never been to a shrine before and I didn't understand why I was being drawn there.

It was a forty-five-minute drive to Beaupré through Quebec City. And what a harrowing ride that was. Kelly drove, Dick navigated, and I just prayed we'd get there in one piece. The streets were narrow, hilly, and made of cobblestone. Dick was trying his best to decipher a French map without being able to read, write, or speak the language. To further confuse things the street signs are in the middle of the street instead of on the corner. We never knew whether we had missed our turn or not. Kelly's instincts, not the map, got us through Old Quebec City and on our way to Beaupré. It was a scenic ride along the St. Lawrence River.

We arrived at Beaupré at 5:45 p.m. At first all we saw was an endless line of tour buses. Then the souvenir shops. I couldn't believe this is what we had come all this way for. We all looked at each other without saying a word. As we turned off of Beaupré Boulevard, we saw the Basilica. It was magnificent! Then I saw the countless steps leading to the entrance of the church and I thought, "Why am I here? I can't even get in." I was afraid that this was like so many other churches at home, inaccessible. But as we turned the corner, I saw the long curved ramp leading to the entrance of the Basilica. What a relief! Dick parked the car while Kelly and I slowly started toward the Basilica. As I breathlessly struggled up the ramp with my leg twisting uncontrollably I felt an excitement building within me. The closer I got to the entrance, the more excited I became.

Kelly held the massive, carved wood door open as I entered the foyer. I began to cry. I felt embarrassed and perplexed. As I walked into the church, my eyes were fixed on two enormous marble pillars on which hung crutches and braces. They had been left by people who had been healed at St. Anne's over the past three hundred years. I began to sob uncontrollably. Kelly helped me to a pew to compose myself. I had no idea why I was crying. I kept telling myself how silly it was to be crying. After all, this was where I wanted to be; there was no need for tears. But I couldn't help myself, the tears kept flowing.

Dick came in at this point and sat in the pew with us. He asked, "What happened? Did you break your foot again?" I said, "No," but I didn't know why I was crying. He didn't say a word, he just sat with me. When I felt more composed, we slowly walked up to the front of the Basilica.

To my left stood the most magnificent statue I have ever seen. It was St. Anne holding her infant daughter, the Blessed Virgin Mary, in her arms. The statue rested on a marble column. As I stood in front of the statue of St. Anne, I was in awe of its beauty. I focused on her face and began to sob even harder. It was as though St. Anne was standing right there with me. This time I didn't question why I was crying. I looked into St. Anne's eyes. I fixed on them. I asked her that if it be her will, to please carry this fear and anxiety for me and give me the inner peace and strength to accept God's will, whatever that may be. At that moment, I felt a tremendous draining from my head to my feet, as though everything was being pulled out of me. I felt the most incredible peace I have ever known. I knew something wonderful had happened. It was as though I was the only person in the Basilica. I think the building could have fallen down around me and I wouldn't have cared or noticed. I walked over to kneel on the marble base at the foot of the statue. Dick tried to stop me, saying, "You can't do that." I hadn't been able to kneel in over fifteen years. I assured him it was okay. While praying, I felt movement in my toes for the first time in six years. They had been frozen in place. Even the doctors were unable to manipulate them to examine me.

I wanted to tell Dick and Kelly. I expected getting up to be difficult but it wasn't. I did it with ease.

I walked over to St. Anne's Altar, directly behind the statue. The railing was covered with flowers, photographs, and petitions. A relic of St. Anne's arm was displayed in a glass-enclosed, gold-trimmed cylinder. Facing the altar, I sat in the pew with Dick and Kelly, telling them that I felt movement in my toes. Kelly suggested that I take my shoe and brace off to see if anything was actually happening. When I did, not only was I able to wiggle my toes but I was also able to rotate my foot at the ankle, something previously impossible to do.

With tears streaming down his face, Dick touched my foot and leg. There was no pain. In a dazed state, Dick wandered away, saying, "This can't be happening. Things like this just don't happen."

Kelly knew immediately what had happened — a miracle. I was in a total state of serenity. I was trying not to make a scene because so many people in the Basilica were praying. Dick, still in a state of shock, continued to wander around the Basilica in tears. He had prayed constantly all these years for me to be free of pain, but the last six years had been an emotional roller coaster. We would no sooner get our hopes up with the prospect of a new treatment than everything would come crashing down with another failure. But this time was different. Deep down, I had always known that God was in control. Acceptance was another story. I am a firm believer that everything happens for a reason. Although that reason may never become known to us in our lifetime, we have to trust in God. But never had I ever considered or asked for a miraculous cure.

I put down my crutches, took off my shoes and brace, and put on Kelly's tennis shoes. I hadn't realized how heavy my orthopedic shoes and brace had been. I walked around the Basilica unaided. At this point all three of us were in tears.

I walked as though I had never had a problem. There was no pain. I had actually put weight on my foot without incurring a fracture. The osteoporosis was gone. I could even take a deep breath without coughing or becoming short of breath. It had been so long, I had forgotten what it felt like to be pain-free or to be able to breathe without feeling as though I had a pillow over my face. I was elated.

Suddenly, I wanted to see a priest. Dick remembered an information station on the ground level of the Basilica. Again, Kelly and I traded shoes, but not before I removed the brace from my orthopedic shoe. I walked out of the Basilica unaided.

Kelly carried my leg brace and Dick carried my crutches. Once outside the Basilica, we could have chosen the steps or the ramp to get to the ground floor. It was an easy decision. I chose the steps. I joyfully walked, almost danced, down them.

We found a shrine aide. Unfortunately he only spoke French and we only spoke English. Dick, Kelly, and I knew some elementary Spanish, but that didn't translate well. Frustrated, he went to find a bilingual-speaking aide, Gerald. Gerald took us into his office and listened as we told him what had happened. He immediately called Father Jacques to come over. While we waited Gerald told us of his eventful thirty-five years of devoted service as a volunteer aide at St. Anne's and the joy that it has brought him.

Word of the healing must have spread quickly. The room began to fill with aides. One of them was chain-smoking. Kelly brought it to my attention. It did not occur to me, as it had to her, how devastating smoke had been to my asthma. All I could say was, "Doesn't it smell awful?" It never bothered my asthma. I knew it, too, was gone.

Father Jacques, a tall, thin Frenchman, arrived after finishing evening Mass. I tearfully recounted the events of the evening. He seemed distant. He listened, but was not excited. When I finished, he apologized for his lack of enthusiasm. Speaking in broken English, he explained that it was not uncommon for people to pretend to be cured from a condition that had never existed. I understood. After all, he didn't know me or my long and complex medical history. He asked us to come back in the morning and we would talk again. We agreed to meet him after the 9:30 a.m. Mass. By this time, it was 8:30 p.m. Emotionally, we were exhausted and still in a state of shock. We decided to get something to eat and return to our hotel.

During the drive to the restaurant, we were in tears one minute and laughing the next, trying to absorb what had happened. Dick was still saying, "How can something like this happen?" I kept looking out the window, hoping to find a shoe store that was still open. I couldn't wait to buy a pair of "normal" shoes.

At the restaurant, the waitress started to light a candle at our table. My first instinct was to stop her, but I decided to see if the asthma really was gone and let her light it. It did not bother me at all, nor did I have any problem with congestion. This was the first meal I had been able to eat without incident in three days.

Back at our hotel, I walked the two flights of stairs with ease. As I prepared for bed, I looked at my night braces for my leg and hands. I decided not to put them on. I trusted in the Lord. I slept soundly all night and had a wonderful dream where I saw my Uncle Heavy, sister Margaret, mother, and mother-in-law just long enough to tell them what had happened. They were so pleased. None of them had lived to see me walk unaided again. This was the first night I slept longer than four hours in the past six years.

When I woke up the next morning I discovered that my foot had not inverted or twisted during the night but was perfectly straight. I had not incurred a fracture. I was completely free of all pain. I had full use of my hands. My breathing was completely normal. The color in my foot and leg had turned from its "normal" bluish color to a healthy pink. The temperature of my foot and leg was now warm instead of cold. Every symptom and characteristic of RSD was gone. I took my first unassisted shower in six years. It was a very long, hot, steamy shower. When I finished, Dick was still muttering, "How can this be?"

Dick and I left the hotel to attend 9:30 a.m. Mass at the Basilica. On the drive to Beaupré, I felt the anxiety building. I had such mixed emotions. I was elated because I was pain-free and unencumbered by my leg brace and crutches. I was full of questions and uncertainty about my future. What would life be like now? What would the doctors say? Before, my life was geared to helping people with disabilities. Now that I didn't have a disability, how effective could I be in advocating for them? How was I going to explain this incredible experience to our family and friends, especially our son, Craig, who hadn't been able to come with us? How was I going to deal with this new life God had given me? I realized that my greatest challenge was going to be how I could best serve God in my new life as a non-disabled person.

As we approached the Basilica, I was shaking. I walked up the steps with ease. The feeling of independence was so new to me I wasn't sure what to make of it. I walked up the center aisle and sat in the front of the church. As I entered a pew, I knelt down and called on St. Anne again. I asked her to please help me by carrying this feeling of anxiety for me. She did, and again an incredible sense of peace came over me. I knew at that moment, my healing was permanent. The realization of God's magnificent gift to me, His power, and His love was overwhelming. A mere thank you seemed so inadequate. Again, the tears came. These were tears of joy and thanksgiving.

After Mass, Dick and I met with Father Jacques. For three hours, between the tears, we gave him the highlights. He took notes and we agreed to mail him my medical history as soon as I could gather it. I was told to send photographs of me in the brace and on crutches, an accounting of the accident, the names, addresses, and specialties of all thirty doctors, an account of the healing, and anything else I felt was pertinent. I was told to see my doctor as soon as possible to confirm the healing.

Father Jacques said there was no doubt in his mind that a miracle had taken place. Dick asked him how frequently this happens. He said it was almost unheard-of for physical healings to take place in this manner. He briefly talked about the process that would take place in order to have my healing declared a miracle by the Church. Once the Basilica received my information, a team of investigators would review it. We were told that this is a lengthy process that could probably take ten years or more. My husband and I looked at each other. We both knew what had happened and that was all that was important.

Father Jacques encouraged us to take the crutches and brace home with us at this time. As we said good-bye, we told him we would return to St. Anne's next year to celebrate and to leave my old brace and crutches to be added to those already hanging on the pillars in the Basilica.

I was touched when Gerald, our new friend, came looking for us. He told us how happy he was for us and wanted to say good-bye. He gave me a hug and a kiss and was off to another day of volunteering at the Basilica.

Leaving the Shrine was very difficult. Although I had only been there two days, I felt so protected and loved, I didn't want to leave, but I knew that I had to; so with tears stream- ing down my face, I walked out of the Ba- silica. But I knew I wasn't walking alone; God was with me as He had been through- out my entire illness. He had never aban- doned me, but rather He em- braced me as I carried my cross.

Little did I know at the time that my

Photo courtesy of Susan Bradford

Daughter Kelly, Susan, Father Jacques, and Dick at St. Anne's, August 12, 1993.

healing would not end here; in fact, my conversion was just beginning. My greatest gift was yet to come — that of knowing the magnificent and incredible love of God the Father, the Son, and the Holy Spirit.

Before leaving, we went to the church store. I hoped to purchase a carved wooden statue of St. Anne de Beaupré, but was disappointed when I wasn't able to find one. As we walked back to our car, I looked around and couldn't help but notice people walking, talking, seeing, hearing, breathing. I wondered if they realized what precious, God-given gifts they possess. I had never allowed myself to think about walking unaided again. I had forgotten what it was like to be completely independent. I never want to forget where I have come from, for it is only through my experiences that I can truly be of service to others.

We arrived back at the hotel at 2 p.m. We rested for a half hour, then drove to beautiful Quebec City to sightsee. The three of us walked up and down the hilly cobblestone streets and in and out of the shops for five hours. I couldn't believe it. I wasn't tired and I had no pain or swelling in my leg or foot.

While walking through the streets of Quebec City, I came upon a small religious-articles store owned by the Sisters of the Magnificat. The Sisters handcraft statues of St. Anne de Beaupré out of clay. As I picked up several of the statues, one in particular felt very warm in my hand. I put it down and continued to look, but I kept coming back to it. Each time I felt that warmth. Naturally, that is the one I purchased. To this day, that statue is warm when I hold it in my hand.

Because of my healing, we decided to cut our vacation short and return home immediately. We were anxious to share our joy with our son, Craig, and the rest of the family. We left for home the next morning. Kelly and Dick decided to drive straight through, fifteen hours. What a ride! So much was going through our minds: How do we explain this to people? Dick still kept pondering how this could happen. We joked, we laughed, and we cried. Kelly decided that her description of the vacation would be "a funny thing happened on vacation, I interviewed at Smith College, we went to a maple syrup factory, and my mother had a miraculous healing." Laughter was finally back in our lives. It felt so good. We arrived home at 1:30 in the morning. We didn't even unpack the car. We went straight to bed.

We awoke early, Dick scrambled through the attic searching for a pair of "normal" shoes for me to wear to 8:30 Mass; it was the Feast of the Assumption. I was very apprehensive walking into church without my braces and crutches, as people had come to know me. It was so strange to walk into my parish church as a non-disabled person. The attendance was relatively low. I was relieved because I wasn't ready to answer too many questions.

When I came out of church one of our associate pastors, Father Waudby, greeted me. He asked what had happened. When I briefly told him, he was overjoyed. He hugged me and kept saying how happy he was for me. He truly understood healing. As it turned out, as a seminarian, he had been very involved in the Healing Ministry of Baltimore, a ministry I was completely unaware of. He understood immediately as I explained. I was so relieved. I don't think he realized the impact that his reaction and understanding had on my transition. I saw our pastor, Monsignor Staub, and briefly explained what happened. I think he was in shock, but then so were we.

On the way home from church, we stopped by my father's house. I needed to be alone with Dad. So Dick dropped me off and went home to call Craig, who was away at college, and ask him to come home; we had something to share with him.

When my father opened the door, I walked in. He didn't say anything at first. With a straight face, he asked, "So, what's new?" I recounted the story of my healing. He hugged me and cried. He said he wished that Mom had lived to see me walk again. I told him that I saw Mom, Margaret, and Uncle Heavy the night I was healed and how happy they were. We both cried.

When Craig arrived home, I was sitting on the sofa. He took

one look at my face and said, "Something has happened. You look completely different." He was so excited when I told him of the healing. It was then that he told me how frightened he was that I was going to die. I shared with him that I was just as scared.

Since my sister Jane lived in California, I had to wait several hours before I could call her. When I told her, I could hear her voice quiver. She asked for a picture of me without the brace and crutches because she had a hard time remembering me without them, and her children had never seen me without them, much less walking unaided.

My sister Monica had moved to England two weeks earlier, so I had no way of getting in touch with her. God's hand was at work again. Monica called me to give me her phone number. She was ecstatic at the news, as were my nieces when I spoke with them. They too had never seen me walk unaided and wanted pictures. We still had many others to share our joy with — Dick's eighty-seven-year-old aunt and his brothers. Everyone was overjoyed.

Monsignor John Kinsella, the pastor of a neighboring church and lifelong friend of Dick's, had been tremendously supportive during my illness. We attended Mass at his church the next morning. When we arrived, John saw us enter the hall. He took one look at me and said, "It's a miracle." We then shared our story. We were honored to be asked to bring up the gifts. I had wanted to do that for years but had been unable.

We celebrated over lunch. Craig joked, saying he would like to have had a t-shirt saying: "My parents went to Quebec. My mom had a miracle, and all I got was this lousy t-shirt." I can't remember all of us laughing so much.

As Father Jacques instructed me, I made an appointment with my orthopedist. I purposely didn't tell the secretary why I wanted to see him, and she was so used to my visits she didn't ask anymore. On September 1, 1992, Dr. Smulyan walked into the examining room, looked for my crutches and brace, and said, "I don't care how you did it, I'm delighted." He was reluctant to touch my foot and leg due to the extreme pain it previously caused. I assured him it was okay. I was no longer in pain. When he examined my foot and leg, he did not find any evidence of the reflex sympathetic dystrophy or the osteoporosis. The deformed leg he was used to treating was now completely straight. I recounted my experience. He said he was very much a believer in faith healing. He told me to call him in a year and let him know how I'm doing. He then discharged me after more than fifteen years of care. Neither of us ever thought that these past years would have a happy ending.

When I returned home, I gathered all my medications and threw them away. They filled an entire trash can to the brim. It was wonderful. I have not needed as much as an aspirin since 6 p.m. on August 12, 1992.

Dick and I began to attend daily Mass as our small way of saying, "Thank you." But again we were on the receiving end. The joy and fulfillment we receive from being in God's presence and receiving the Eucharist daily is unsurpassed. God gives us the opportunity to be with Him every day and to witness the greatest miracle of all times, that of the Consecration. I am to this day overwhelmed when the bread and wine are consecrated into the Body and Blood of Jesus Christ. I know that the Eucharist is not a mere symbol, but the living, breathing body of Jesus Christ. I am given the opportunity and the privilege of receiving Him daily. I cannot imagine starting my day in any other way.

Trying to process my healing, I went to the library. I was sure I would find books written on miracles such as mine. I could find only one, *Miracles Do Happen,* by Sister Breige McKenna. I really felt supported. As Sister Breige was healed in very much the same manner as I had been. I have spoken to many priests whose reactions have varied from "I don't understand healing" to "That's wonderful" to "You need to share your story." All have rejoiced with me in the goodness of the Lord. Monsignor Kinsella suggested that I meet with Father

Larry Gesy, who directed the healing Ministry of Baltimore and would be able to walk me through my transition. John was right, Father Larry was and is today immensely supportive and understanding of my spiritual growth.

In early October, I was feeling very apprehensive and I didn't understand why. Physically I felt great. I was walking again. I could breath with ease, and my osteoporosis was gone. Still, I felt those old fears and anxieties coming back; I was literally shaking. I decided to lie down for a while. As I reached for something to read, I noticed the three rosaries lying in my night table drawer. One had belonged to my sister, one to my mother-in-law, and the other was mine. They had lain there untouched for years. As I held each in my hand I felt a particular warmth, almost heat, from my mother-in-law's rosary. I decided to pray the Rosary. As I prayed, I felt a sense of total peace and calmness come over me. By the third decade, I heard a voice say, "You just don't know how to be healthy." I understood right away. I had lived with ill health for over fifteen years. I didn't know how to let it go. That afternoon my next-door neighbor called to see how I was doing. The first thing she said was, "It must be hard getting used to being healthy." She was so right. I think this was God's way of saying, "If you didn't get My message the first time, here is a reminder."

That began my love of the Rosary. Months of praying the Rosary passed when one Sunday morning, I noticed something written on the back of the crucifix. Dick read it for me. It said: "Sainte Anne de Beaupré." Dick's mother had never been to St. Anne's. To this day we have no idea where the rosary came from. There is an incredible feeling of peace, comfort, and love that comes from praying the Rosary .

On October first, I woke up feeling a lot of sensation at the injury site on my leg. It is hard to describe the feeling, since I had never felt anything like this. It wasn't pain. I wasn't sure what was going on, but I wasn't concerned. It continued all day and throughout the evening. When I awoke the next morning, I discovered that the graft area had not only faded but the deep indentation in my leg had begun to fill in.

In early November, Dick and I drove to the Grotto of Our Lady of Lourdes in Emmitsburg, Maryland. What a marvelous presence of peace and love at the Grotto. When I walked into the Chapel of Mary, I could hear myself singing the Hail Holy Queen. As I knelt before the statue of Mary, I began to cry. Again I felt a surge in my leg and realized that more changes had taken place. God's hand was still working. When I looked down, the scars had almost disappeared. It was then that I asked God not to take them all from me. I didn't ever want to forget my illness and how merciful God had been to me. The scars I once was so ashamed of I couldn't be prouder of today. I didn't understand all that was happening or why. I had an incredible sense of joy, as though God were dwelling within me.

On August 12, 1993, we returned to St. Anne's to participate in a Mass of thanksgiving on the one-year anniversary of my healing. Father Jacques asked me to give witness to my healing at the Mass. He said I would have five minutes. I said, "Yes." I had no idea of how I was going to compress everything into five minutes. I turned to Jesus. I asked Him to give me the words to deliver the message that He wanted delivered. As I stood in front of six hundred people, I didn't know what I was going to say. I trusted that Jesus was with me. The words came, and five minutes later, I had delivered a message of hope and love. Jesus never lets us down.

At the offertory, Dick, Kelly, and I brought up the gifts. My gift was to return my crutches and brace back to the Lord. When I handed them to Father Jacques, I said, "It's over. It's finally over." My journey did not end here: in fact it was just beginning. Little did I know that my healing had not been completed in Canada.

I have learned to put all things in perspective; of what is really important in life and what is not. It's not material possessions, financial wealth, knowing the right people, shopping trips,

owning expensive cars. It's being able to tell the difference between what we need and what we want. Our needs are very
basic. It's our wants and desires that get us in trouble. But, I
know that it is our relationship with God and how we serve Him
that must be our priority in life. It's about faith, hope, and love.
We are not here on earth for personal gain but for service to
God in whatever way He wants to use us.

I am learning patience in everything that I do. This has been
very hard for me because of my tendency to want immediate
results. God works in His time, not ours. I must recognize this
and work toward patience in everything I do.

The Scriptures have taken on a new meaning for me. I never
took the time to read them or even listen closely to them at
Mass. I now pray for understanding as I reflect on them. What
I have come to realize is that they are as relevant today as they
were two thousand years ago. They come alive and give meaning to our lives as Christians. It is unfortunate that my generation was not encouraged to read or to gain an understanding of
Scriptures.

The Lord has led me to the healing ministry. I call this ministry the best-kept secret of the Catholic Church. I never knew
such a ministry existed prior to my healing. Yet Scriptures are
very clear. We are told in Corinthians 12:7-10: "To each individual the manifestation of the Spirit is given for some benefit.
To one is given . . . gifts of healing by the Spirit. . . ." Through
the laying on of hands of this ministry, I have seen people healed
in many ways. Spiritually, emotionally, and physically. The
power of prayer is incredible. Scripture again tells us, "For
where two or three are gathered in my name, there am I in the
midst of them" (Mt 18:20).

I have come to realize that when people pray for a cure, ask
where God is, or get angry because their prayers are not being
answered the way they think they should be, they are in fact
asking for what *they* want from God, not what God wants for
them. We are asked to trust Him and surrender to His will. But

one thing I am certain of is that whenever we ask, God heals us according to His will, not ours. I've seen people healed as they lay on their deathbed, others who are looking for peace and strength in their lives, some with terminal diseases sent into total remission, and some with no signs of the illness. Sometimes it is helping someone to prepare to go home to the Lord or to overcome addictions. Many times it is helping someone to forgiveness and to go past anger. The list is endless. Often we are, through our illnesses, used as instruments of healing for family members. Jesus invites us to carry our cross with Him.

I know that God is the most powerful force in my life. My only regret is that it took me so long to find Him. I will always be grateful to Him for all the blessings and graces He has bestowed upon me. Yes, even for the accident and the more than fifteen years of suffering and illness that followed. I learned so much during that time. I can now thank God for everything in my life, the good and the bad.

Before my healing I never knew or understood why things were happening in my life; however, I knew that I had to trust in God's wisdom. Even when I was at my worst, I never felt that I was walking alone but knew that God was always with me. I understand now that He knows what is best for me and for everyone. Although at times it may seem profoundly unfair and even unjust, some of us are asked to endure more than others. Jesus invites us to carry our cross with Him while giving us the strength and courage to do so. We often have to go through very difficult times to recognize God's presence in our lives. I believe God tests our love for Him. We are all tested in some way. God's love teaches us the love and value of family, to be sensitive to others in need, how to forgive others, and to live with life's trials in hope and love.

As I look back, I don't know that I could have learned these lessons of love without first having to carry my own cross. I have learned that with Jesus in my life all things are possible. Above all — never, never give up hope.

Jesus suffered and died because He loves every one of us. When we are open to Him and ask Him into our lives, He fills us with faith, hope, love, peace, and strength. He has shown me a love far greater than human love, one that I never knew existed. He has shown me that Catholicism is a way of life, not just reserved for one hour on Sunday morning. He has molded me, guided me, and protected me. "I am with you always," says the Lord.

The Lord has led me to many new paths since my healing,

Father Larry Gesy and Susan

but one special path that I follow every day is to a ministry with the Franciscan Center, an emergency outreach center for God's special people, those who live in poverty. There are so many correlations between the life of Christ and that of the poor it is no wonder that God loves them so. "Blessed are you who are poor, for the kingdom of God is yours" (Lk 6:20).

The Lord always knows what I need and provides for me. He has been my friend, my teacher, my advisor. He has opened the doors He wanted opened, when He wanted them opened by always putting the right people in my path. Recently he brought me the gift of a spiritual director, Father Jack Collopy. I knew Father Jack as a child when he served as an assistant to my Uncle Heavy, who was the pastor at St. Andrew's Church in Baltimore. The Lord reunited Father Jack and me, so that I

Photo courtesy of Susan Bradford

Susan's crutches are among those that hang from the marble pillars at St. Anne's.

could have an earthly guide to walk me through my daily conversion and battles against the evil one. I have learned that I must be patient. When the time is right, the Lord will tell me and guide me to where He wants me to be.

I continue to go back to St. Anne de Beaupré's every year to say thank you. My crutches now hang on the marble pillars in the church. Each time I have entered the church and have been greeted with the sight of these pillars and my old crutches has been an emotional experience. These crutches were once my only source of mobility, but now they are a reminder of God's mercy and love. Through the grace of God and the intercession of Mary and St. Anne, I was healed.

My conversion is ongoing. The richness of my spirituality deepens every day as I nurture and attend to it, much like workers in the vineyard who nurture the grapes that will make a fine wine. For the harvest to be bountiful, the workers must attend to and care for the grapes daily; and for us to realize the full greatness of God we must attend to our spiritual needs each and every day of our lives. God gave me a tremendous gift. My physical healing was the shiny, pretty package, but my spiritual healing was the greatest gift I have ever received.

Dolores M. White

"Why my little girl?"

I married in 1978 and wanted to start a family right away, as I had always hoped for and looked forward to having children. A few months later I became pregnant, but when I was two months along I had a bad hemorrhage. My husband rushed me to the hospital where the doctors told me that I had lost one baby of twins. They were certain that I would lose the other, unless I would get off my feet and rest in bed for days. I did, and seven months later gave birth to a beautiful, healthy baby girl, whom we named Joyce.

A year later I became pregnant again, and again hemorrhaged two months later. My doctor told me that I had a tendency to miscarry during the first trimester of pregnancy. I had stayed off my feet and rested in bed, but miscarried anyway. Even though the doctor tested carefully, he could find nothing wrong to explain why I tended to bleed so profusely. He advised me to wait a few months before becoming pregnant again because I had given birth to Joyce by Caesarian section.

A few months later I became pregnant again, and soon hemorrhaged. I went to bed, remained there a week, and the bleeding stopped. Three days later, the bleeding recurred so I returned to bed. Finally, after seven months I gave birth by Caesarian section to our second child, Julie Anne.

We had been planning for a third child, but wanted to move from our house because the neighborhood was changing rapidly. Some of our neighbors used drugs, some drank heavily, some abused their small children, and most seemed to worship material things. We even had to change our phone number because of crank calls.

Since Joyce had no playmates among the neighbors and could not safely play in our yard because our street had heavy traffic, we decided to enroll her in nursery school. She liked playing with her classmates. She was happy. Then one morning Joyce said she didn't feel well, so I kept her at home. She played all day with her little sister. I watched her go to her room, put on a flowered dress — and lipstick. From the top of the TV, she picked up her picture as an infant, smiled, and said, "Easter."

Later that evening Joyce became very sick, vomited, and went into convulsions. We rushed her to the hospital by ambulance, but she died four hours later, September 30, 1982. The diagnosis was that she had died of meningitis caused by *hemophilus influenza*, a common but often fatal infection of children between the ages of two and five. It can cause death or brain damage. At the time, no vaccine was available to prevent her illness and death.

Julie Anne was only a year old, but even though meningitis is very contagious she did not become sick. (In 1985, a vaccine became available, not the best, but it gave some protection to Julie Anne. A better vaccine was developed in 1987.)

When I said to a Catholic priest whom I met at the hospital that God had taken Joyce from me, he replied that, "No, God did not take her away; a fatal illness took her away." We were devastated: lonely, empty, sad, fearful. I kept asking: "Why? Why us? Why my little girl?"

Three weeks later I was invited to a religious gathering. Those present were praying aloud and praising God. During the evening, while I was seated, someone laid hands on my head. I felt something like electricity go through my body, and said in a voice unlike my own, "Come to me. I love you." I was filled with the Holy Spirit. Someone was praying in tongues and I was praying in tongues too. I was in a state of intense joy and delight, happy and at peace. I did not know what was happening. Someone told me that I had been "baptized in the Holy Spirit." I was raised Catholic, and never missed Sunday Mass. This seemed different from the Catholicism with which I had been familiar.

When I went home that night, I picked up my Bible to read some of my favorite passages. The Scriptures became my consolation, joy, and comfort in my grief. Jesus took me out of the darkness and gave me His light. The more I read the more I was able to understand. One of my favorite verses is from the Sermon on the Mount: "Blessed are they who mourn, for they will be comforted" (Mt 5:4). Another is from Psalm 27: "The Lord is my light and my salvation; whom should I fear?" I am strongly attracted to the Gospel of St. Luke, too.

I also attended a charismatic prayer group in our parish, but I needed to learn to beware of false prophets. At one point during our time of grief, some people came to our door saying that they had been sent by God. They stayed for dinner with us, but later we discovered that they were not Christians.

I kept thinking: Life is precious; life is a wonderful gift. God gave us life, this most valuable gem. Joyce is very special to God in heaven.

A few months later I became pregnant. I was worried about hemorrhaging and fearful of losing this baby. Then a friend told me about Father Larry Gesy's healing Masses at St. Anthony's Church, a ministry that he had started there in 1983. Until that time I had not been to a Mass followed by a healing service. At the last moment, I decided to go. I was nervous because I did not know what to expect and I was apprehensive about experiencing evening sickness because I was two months pregnant. For those reasons and because the church was very crowded, with long lines of people attending, I stood at the back of the church, very close to the back wall.

The Gospel read at the Mass before the healing service was Luke 8:43-44:

> And a woman afflicted with hemorrhages for twelve years who [had spent her whole livlihood on doctors and] was unable to be cured by anyone, came up behand him and touched the tassel on his cloak. Immediately her bleeding stopped.

I am very shy, but I felt a hand holding my hand and I heard a voice saying, "Go!" but it was not a real person holding my hand and talking to me. I went through the crowd and across the lines of people to the altar. Father Larry was facing the other way, so he did not see me. I touched his vestment, the edge of his robe. I had a lot of faith, and at that moment I believed with all my heart that I would be healed. Physically, mentally, spiritually, emotionally, I *was* healed! I was at peace! Like the woman in Luke's Gospel, no more bleeding. Father Larry turned and looked at me and blessed me. Praise Jesus! Through Christ the Healer I was healed!

When I returned home and told my husband he was very happy. The next day I cleaned my house, did the laundry, picked up Julie Anne, shopped for groceries, all with no bleeding! During the next few months we had three yard sales, still no bleeding. Through the entire pregnancy I did not need bed rest. It was the only one of my pregnancies during which I did not hemorrhage.

Seven months after the healing Mass I gave birth to a beautiful, normal baby girl whom we named Theresa Elizabeth. She is nine-and-a-half years old now and will be in the fifth grade this September.

After Theresa was born I returned to another healing service at St. Anthony's to tell Father Larry about my new baby girl. At the Mass that night, he read Luke 8:43-44 and announced my healing.

I had prayed that Joyce's death would be the means of bringing some people to the Lord. It has come about. Friends, relatives, and neighbors have turned to Jesus, not only because of Joyce, but also because of the healing they saw take place for me. God always keeps his promises. Thanks be to God. Thanks to Jesus.

Linda Gagalski

Divine mercy in my life

Three o'clock was the hour of agony for Jesus on the cross. At that moment "Blood and water . . . gushed forth from the Heart of Jesus as a fount of mercy for us. . . ." (*Diary of Blessed Faustina*, 309).

At exactly that same hour on Friday, May 21, 1993, my world was shattered. When a state police trooper and a Social Service worker came to my door, a thousand panicky thoughts ran through my mind: Who's hurt? Trish . . . Katrina . . . Bill. . . . ? Was there an accident? Injury? Illness? My mind raced with dread and my heart was breaking before I even knew what had happened. But the one thought I never imagined was that there was no accident, no injury during normal child's play, no dangerous stranger.

Instead, I learned of something even more unthinkable: a five-year period of deliberate sexual abuse against my youngest daughter, Katrina, by the trusted husband of my day-care provider who was a close friend of eleven years, the man who was my children's designated guardian in our will. The pain I felt at that three o'clock hour was excruciating.

You see, earlier that same morning in school Katrina handed in an anonymous note to a state trooper visiting her class. The note said, "If a friend of yours had been sexually abused what should she do?" Of course, a note like this from a sixth grader usually covers up a personal problem. The trooper asked that the student who had written this note please privately come forward. And that's when Katrina disclosed her abuse for the first time.

My oldest daughter, Trish, began in this day-care provider's home at the age of one. Their family and ours became fast friends and family-like in our relationship. We spent holidays, First Communions, graduations, birthdays, and almost all family gatherings together. We quickly came to love these people, trusting them implicitly with our daughters. In fact, my husband, Bill, and I asked them if they would be guardians of our girls in our will. We felt so blessed to have such wonderful people caring for our children while we worked. In a time when good day care was so hard to come by we perceived ourselves fortunate.

Trish and Katrina loved their "second home." Sometimes they would even spend weekend nights there because they'd have so much fun. Then, after many years in this nurturing environment, Ed (the day-care husband) took five-year-old Katrina to his bedroom. That began a five-year period of sexual abuse which took place a few times each week.

As a baby and toddler, Katrina was a feisty, happy-go-lucky little girl whose laughter was contagious. I remember teasing her kindergarten teacher that she'd have her hands full with Katrina. Her love of life might be hard to contain in a classroom. But her exuberance stilled. Her teacher described her as shy and quiet. She said that possibly Katrina had just matured once she began school. Now I know that her abuse began sometime before kindergarten.

In subsequent years Katrina needed me much more than Trish seemed to. Bill and I always strived to provide both our girls with a stable, safe, loving home. Yet Katrina, for then unknown reasons, couldn't go up to her bed without Mommy or Daddy staying with her. She couldn't take a shower without one of us remaining upstairs, and she frequently wakened screaming during the night from a nightmare she never remembered. Looking back now, the molestation imposed on her explains everything. In our naïve world, Bill and I were only concerned that Katrina might be extra sensitive. So, thank God, we instinctively comforted Katrina all those years, even "babied" her as Trish would see it. We never imagined the hell that Katrina was going through in the home of our trusted care-giver and friend.

On that beautiful, warm afternoon in May, 1993, darkness descended on my world at three o'clock. After about a half-hour of a total, icy numbness, I fell apart. Phoning my husband and parents, I became hysterical. Trying to talk between deep, gut-wrenching sobs was impossible. "My baby," I kept thinking. "My baby . . . Oh my God! My baby!" When it seemed as if I had no more remaining tears, I'd cry some more, then I'd sink into despair and desolation. It felt as if someone close to me had died. I was grieving for Katrina's lost childhood.

Questioned by the police, Ed confessed immediately. His statement of facts was fairly identical to Katrina's statement. Even with his admission of guilt it still took six long months to go through the court system. He pleaded guilty, so Katrina was thankfully spared testifying in open court.

I can't describe how much I looked forward to Ed's day of sentencing. I wanted revenge. Bill, Trish, Katrina, and I had done everything in our power to put him in jail for as long as possible. We worked closely with our state attorney's office to see justice accomplished. We begged the judge to give a very stiff sentence. After all, Katrina had been given a life sentence of painful memories the day Ed had first touched her.

The judge was very compassionate toward us. He seemed to have a good sense of the loss our family had experienced. In words validating Katrina's self-worth, the judge handed down a fifteen-year jail term with eleven years suspended, four served.

Also, he imposed a five-year supervised probation upon Ed's release from incarceration. This sentence was even stronger than what our state attorney had argued for. Unexpectedly, though, I wasn't elated at this outcome. Yes, I definitely felt relieved, but was that also a hint of sympathy for Ed in my heart? He had asked for our forgiveness in a letter handed to the judge. And as he was handcuffed and led out of court, I experienced a myriad of emotions that I couldn't comprehend.

The following three months are only a hazy memory now. Our closest friends and family thought our lives had returned to normal. I didn't have the foggiest idea what normal was any more! Katrina was still in individual and group therapies but we no longer had a court date hanging over us. I had learned to hide all my emotions to blend in with the rest of my family. They preferred not to discuss Ed, the abuse, or its effects on all of us; but I could have talked unceasingly.

In suppressing my true emotions, the pain began to backlash. I had frequent crying spells, difficulty sleeping, and trouble with concentration and memory. Worst of all, I kept "seeing" Ed everywhere. At every turn — in church, on television, in every store — I saw his face. When I'd be driving, I'd even think that every little red car was his. Obsession had taken control of my life. Through therapy I discovered that I was experiencing something called "secondary post-traumatic stress syndrome." In other words, even though the trauma of sexual abuse had not occurred to me, I was experiencing most of the same symptoms because of my close relationship with my daughter.

My spiritual life, as you can imagine, was in terrible turmoil. As a Eucharistic minister I felt tremendous guilt about my feelings of hatred and revenge. Until then, I had thought of myself as a fairly good Catholic who could forgive most anything. But my pain was too unbearable to allow forgiveness in this circumstance. So every time I prayed the Our Father my version went like this: "Forgive us our trespasses as we forgive those who trespass against us . . . Okay, God, you can hold one against me!" It really hurt to pray the Our Father because I had to alter it to accommodate my unwillingness to forgive Ed.

I once sought the advice of a particularly compassionate priest at Katrina's school. He reassured me of God's love and understanding of a mother's pain. He asked me to lift my heart to God, ask *Him* to forgive Ed since I wasn't able to. After all, on the cross, Jesus called out, "*Father*, forgive them. . . " (Lk 23:34). It took a few weeks of many false starts before I could sincerely ask God to forgive Ed. At least it was a first step for me. My Our Father, though, remained painfully the same. And my depression deepened with time.

A few months later our parish was sent a new pastor, Father Larry Gesy, well known for his work in the healing ministry. "How perfect!" I thought. Still searching for spiritual peace, I spoke with Father Larry about Katrina's abuse and the darkness left surrounding me. Admittedly, I wasn't too pleased when Father reminded me of Jesus' full request on the cross: "Father forgive them, *they know not what they do*" (Lk 23:34 [italics added]). He said Ed's actions were caused by a sickness, pedophilia. And if I'd try to keep in mind that it was indeed an illness, I could more easily find forgiveness for the person behind the actions. I understood what Father Larry was saying but he was pushing me beyond my comfort level! "After all," I thought, "Ed *did* know what he was doing to my Katrina!" Leaving the rectory after talking with my pastor an uneasiness began to take the place of depression.

When Father Larry organized a pilgrimage bus trip to our archdiocesan shrine of The Divine Mercy at Holy Rosary Church in Baltimore, Maryland, Katrina asked me if we could go. Reluctantly, for her sake I agreed. During the hour ride to the church we watched a documentary film, "Divine Mercy — No Escape," which was about Blessed Faustina and her devotion to Divine Mercy.

Sister Faustina was a young, uneducated Polish nun who in the 1930s received a message of mercy from the Lord. In obedience to her spiritual director she recorded over six hundred pages of divine revelations about God's mercy. She lived a cheerful and humble existence, suffering greatly in silence with tuberculosis. In 1938 at the age of thirty-three, Sister Faustina died. Her writings are contained in the book *Divine Mercy in My Soul—Diary*. In 1993 she was beatified under Pope John Paul II and is presently a candidate for canonization.

Not having heard of any of this before, I was curiously interested. In the film, Dr. Robert Schuller gave a definition of "mercy." "Mercy — what is it? Mercy is really love in action — for people who don't deserve it. For once they deserve it — it's justice!" My heart leapt when I heard this. It seemed as if the documentary was meant only for me. That definition of "mercy" kept repeating over and over in my head. And I somehow knew that the answer to my prayers and finding peace in the midst of my agony was close!

Once at church, we had a few minutes before Mass, Benediction, and the Chaplet of Divine Mercy (intercessory prayers usually sung and prayed on ordinary rosary beads). So I chose to use this spare time for the Sacrament of Reconciliation. In the confessional I admitted to my pastor, Father Larry, that I had not yet been able to forgive the man who had molested my daughter. I also told him that "this Divine Mercy thing" was stirring something inside of me. Father Larry told me that he was certain that I was led to the Shrine of Divine Mercy for a very special reason. For my penance I was to listen very closely to everything said during these services.

The message of Divine Mercy as told to Blessed Faustina when Jesus appeared to her during the 1930s was threefold: to turn to Him with trust, to ask for His Mercy, and to be "merciful to others by our actions . . . words, and . . . prayers" ("The Message of Divine Mercy" pamphlet, Marian Helpers, 1993). When Jesus appeared to Blessed Faustina, rays of red and pale light streamed from the area around His heart. The rays represented the blood and water which flowed from His pierced side.

And similar to the scene on Easter Sunday night, His right hand was raised in blessing (see John 20:19-23). Jesus asked Blessed Faustina to have this vision painted along with the words, "Jesus, I trust in You." He said, "I am offering people a vessel with which they are to keep coming for graces to the fountain of mercy. That vessel is this image with the signature: 'Jesus, I trust in you' " (*Diary*, 327).

After the consecration, as I prayed the Our Father I felt enveloped in God's mercy. "Jesus, I trust in You. Jesus, I do forgive Ed." It was such a simple, pure thought. And completely freeing! Then I heard a voice in my head say, "Go to the prison to see him." "Oh God, no!" I thought. "Not that! Please don't ask me to do that!" I knew, though, that God had indeed asked me to go see Ed and witness to the power of Divine Mercy. "When a soul approaches Me with trust, I fill it with such an abundance of graces that it cannot contain them within itself, but radiates them to other souls" (*Diary*, 1074).

I stumbled upon every possible obstacle that could keep me from visiting the prison. First, I had to get my name on Ed's visitor's list, which I did by writing him a brief note. Father Larry agreed to accompany me for spiritual support, and the morning we were to leave he was delayed by an urgent visitor. Rushing, we arrived at the prison after an hour's drive only to go to the wrong location, then to have the iron gates close as we approached because visitors' hour was over! I was in tears, scared, and confused. "Was I not supposed to do this?" It was becoming more than I could handle emotionally!

It would be another hour before I could go in — more anxious waiting and fretting over what I'd actually say to Ed. Father Larry was a much-needed, calming presence. He reminded me that God would give me the right words to say (cf. Jeremiah 1:6-9) since I was there for all the right reasons.

When the time came, I left Father Larry in the waiting area and was taken through two locked, heavy doors that clanged shut behind me. I froze on entering the prisoner meeting room.

It wasn't at all as I had imagined, with glass panels to separate us and phones to talk through as I'd seen on TV. Instead, this was one massive room filled with easy chairs facing each other! I was so frightened of the unknown that I just trembled. A guard told me where to be seated, and time passed excruciatingly slowly. Then I saw Ed enter the room, looking fifteen years older than he had six months earlier in court. When he spotted me, he approached cautiously. I was not allowed to move from my seat and everything seemed to stir in slow motion . . . until Ed was in front of me. I instinctively pulled him close as we both sobbed into each other's shoulder. I then reached for his hands, clenching them in mine, as we sat facing one another.

I honestly don't remember much of what I said to him. I remember him breaking down again as he told me how sorry he was for hurting Katrina, my family, and for destroying our relationship with his family. He said he had prayed for us daily. I told him I forgave him and asked if he understood that *God* had forgiven him because he was truly remorseful. "The greater the sinner, the greater the right he has to My mercy" (*Diary*, 723). Then I cried again as I apologized to him for taking so long to grant him the forgiveness he had asked for. Still our hands remained joined and I could feel the powerful energy of Divine Mercy flowing between us in the presence of the Lord. "Jesus, I trust in you; Ed, I forgive you; Ed, I ask for your forgiveness." These were the unspoken words that were just as real as any I did say. A gentle calm descended on me, the response of Divine Mercy — a healing power that transcends all human logic. "Mankind will have no peace until it turns with trust to My mercy!" (*Diary*, 300). "Blessed are the merciful for they shall be shown mercy" (Mt 5:7).

I had a curious experience the following week when I had the privilege of attending a large-scale Marian conference. As a Eucharistic minister I was honored by Father Larry's request to bring our parish's monstrance and consecrated Host of Jesus to the conference for Friday evening's liturgy. Since Father Larry

Gesy was the conference emcee and celebrant of the Friday evening Benediction and healing service, he had asked me to personally bring and look after our monstrance. It is very historic, and he was concerned about its security.

It seemed fitting when the conference opened at three o'clock Friday afternoon with the Chaplet of Divine Mercy. It was a very spiritual day and it was so refreshing to be able to pray wholeheartedly. My only regret was that I wouldn't be returning for the second day because of my work schedule.

At midnight, when I returned the monstrance and Host to my church I was shocked. I had brought the wrong one back! It looked just like our monstrance except in the four carved metal faces that surrounded the Host. Our monstrance had four of the *same* faces surrounding the Host. They were all of Jesus with a very gentle expression and soft flowing hair. This monstrance had four *different* carved faces — those of Matthew, Mark, Luke, and John. None of them even resembled the face of Jesus I had seen for months at our weekly parish Benediction services!

Embarrassed, I had to go back to the Marian conference on Saturday to return the Blessed Sacrament encased in this other monstrance. My embarrassment reached an all-time peak, though, when the sacristan informed me it was indeed my own parish monstrance! The night before, Father Larry had told him all about the history of it and the four separate faces of the Gospel writers. "What is wrong with me?" I thought. "How could I have been so mistaken . . . and foolish?" I decided to stay for the remainder of the evening even though I felt like hiding under a rock. I kept wondering how I could have been so wrong! Only a few moments later, I had my answer. In a brief conversation with a new acquaintance, I found myself sharing with and ministering to this person who had also been through an experience of sexual abuse. Then it dawned on me! I hadn't been dragging Jesus (in the most Blessed Sacrament) all around town. He had been dragging me around to get me back here! I was meant to be at this Marian conference at this moment for someone else's sake. Forgiving Ed and going to prison to see him had not been an ending to my story. Clearly it was a beginning for me!

I can't say whether or not a miracle had caused me to see for months the four different faces on our monstrance as one and the same of Jesus. My pastor, Father Larry Gesy, and I only know that there definitely seemed to be a purpose in it for me.

A month after the conference, I went back to our archdiocesan shrine of The Divine Mercy. On the anniversary of Blessed Faustina's death, there was a special service being held. A painting was also on display that was the first copy of the original painting of Jesus, "The Divine Mercy," as described to an artist by Blessed Faustina. I was quite drawn to this image because of the impact of Divine Mercy in my life. Leaving the church at the end of the evening. I purchased a print of that specific image and held it as I stopped to speak to Father Ron Pytel, pastor of Holy Rosary Church. He knew of my experience with the power of Divine Mercy and of my prison visit, so I proceeded to tell him my "monstrance story." At the part about how I had always seen only one face — that of a very gentle-looking Jesus, I looked down at the picture of Divine Mercy in my hand and exclaimed, "Oh my God! *This* is the face I saw!"

It was indeed the exact image of Jesus as The Divine Mercy which for months had been so very real to me in our parish monstrance.

Jesus, I do trust in You!

(At the request of my daughter, the young victim in the preceding story, the names of my family members have been changed. I'd like to give special thanks to Father Larry Gesy for his spiritual, emotional, and physical support and for leading me toward my devotion to The Divine Mercy. May the love and divine mercy of Jesus bless every aspect of your life.
— *Linda Gagalski*)

With permission by the Marian Helpers, the following is reprinted from their pamphlet about The Divine Mercy.

The Message of Divine Mercy: Trust in Mercy and Be Merciful

The Message

The Message of Divine Mercy is that God is merciful. He is love itself poured out for us, and He wants no one to escape that merciful love.

The message is that God wants us to turn to Him with trust and repentance while it is still a time of mercy, before He comes as the just judge. This turning with trust to Him who is Mercy is the only source of peace for mankind. Turning to and imploring God's mercy is the answer to the troubled world. There is no escaping that answer.

The Response of Trust and Conversion

What God most wants of us is to turn to Him with trust. And the first act of trust is to receive His mercy. To trust God is to rely on Him who is Mercy itself. The Lord wants us to live with trust in Him in all circumstances. We trust Him because He is God, and He loves us and cares for us. His mercy is always available to us, no matter what we have done or what state we are in, even in our sins are as black as night and we are filled with fears and anxieties.

"The greater the sinner, the greater the right he has to My mercy" (*Diary of Blessed Faustina*, 723).

The Response of Mercy Toward Others

Not only are we to receive His mercy, but we are to use it, being merciful to others by our action, by our words, and by our prayers; in other words by practicing the Corporal and Spiritual Works of Mercy.

The Corporal Works of Mercy are feeding the hungry, giving drink to the thirsty, clothing the naked, sheltering the travelers, comforting the prisoners, visiting the sick, and burying the dead. The Spiritual Works of Mercy include teaching the ignorant, praying for the living and the dead, correcting sinners, consoling the sorrowful, bearing wrongs patiently, and forgiving wrongs willingly.

It's Scriptural

The message of mercy is the content and the challenge of Sacred Scripture. In the Hebrew Bible we see a God of mercy who calls His people to be merciful. In the New Testament Jesus exhorts us:

Be merciful, even as your Father is merciful (Lk 6:36 RSV).

He sets the highest goal for us and expects us to obtain it by His merciful love:

Blessed are the merciful, for they shall obtain mercy (Mt 5:7 RSV).

When He comes again, He will judge us on our mercy toward one another:

Truly, I say to you, as you did it to one of the least of these my brethren, you did it to me (Mt 25:40 RSV).

It's the Current Teaching of Pope John Paul II

The message of The Divine Mercy — Jesus Himself — is at the heart of the Gospel. The message of mercy presents the truth and the call of the Gospel to our present age. This message of mercy is proclaimed by Pope John Paul II, in his encyclical *Rich in Mercy* (*Dives in miseridcordia*, November 30, 1980), as the message for our age.

". . . The Church must consider it one of her principle duties — at every stage of history and especially in our modern age — to *proclaim and to introduce into life* the mystery of mercy, supremely revealed in Jesus Christ" (14) [italics added].

Mercy — The Message and Response Through the Ages

The message and response of mercy is not something new. In the past, God spoke à message of mercy through the patriarchs and prophets — through Noah, Abraham, Moses, Elijah, and many others.

In the last days God has spoken to us by His Son, Jesus Christ, who is Mercy personified and incarnated.

God continues to speak a word of mercy even to our generation, through the Church and its shepherds, and through holy men and women — mystics — whom God has chosen as His vessels.

In our century He revealed Himself to Blessed Faustina, a simple and holy nun in Poland during the 1930s. He called her to be His secretary and His apostle of mercy. He spoke to her of His mercy and the way He wants us to respond to it.

Devotion to The Divine Mercy

Our Lord not only taught Blessed Faustina the fundamentals of trust, and mercy to others, but He also revealed special ways to live out the response to His mercy. These we call the "devotion to The Divine Mercy." The word "devotion" means fulfilling our vows. It is a commitment of our lives to the Lord who is Mercy itself.

By giving our lives to The Divine Mercy — Jesus Christ Himself — we become instruments of His mercy to others, and so we can live out the command of the Lord:

Be merciful, even as your Father is merciful (Lk 6:36 RSV).

Through Blessed Faustina, Our Lord gave us special means of drawing on His mercy: an Image of The Divine Mercy, a Chaplet of Divine Mercy, a Feast of Mercy, a novena, and prayer at the three o'clock hour — the hour of His death.

These special means are in addition to the Sacraments of Eucharist and Reconciliation, which have been given to the Church.

The Image of The Divine Mercy

Jesus appeared to Blessed Faustina with rays of red and pale light streaming from the area around His heart. His right hand was raised in blessing, recalling the scene of Easter Sunday night (see John 20:19-23).

He asked Blessed Faustina to have this vision painted along with the words, "Jesus, I trust in You!"

He presented this image to remind people to trust in His mercy, and to come to Him for mercy:

"I am offering people a vessel with which they are to keep coming for graces to the fountain of mercy. That vessel is this image with the signature: 'Jesus, I trust in You' " (*Diary*, 327).

Jesus explained that the rays represented the blood and water which flowed from His pierced side, and He taught Blessed Faustina the prayer:

"O Blood and Water, which gushed forth from the Heart of Jesus as a fountain of mercy for us, I trust in You" (*Diary*, 84).

The Chaplet of The Divine Mercy

Our Lord taught Blessed Faustina a prayer for mercy that she was to pray "unceasingly": The Chaplet of The Divine Mercy.

He told her that, if she prayed in this way, her prayers would have great power for the conversion of sinners, for peace for the dying, and even for controlling nature.

We, too, can pray this chaplet, using ordinary rosary beads of five decades. We begin with the Our Father, the Hail Mary, and the Apostles Creed.

Then, on the large beads we pray:

"Eternal Father, I offer you the Body and Blood, Soul and Divinity of Your Dearly Beloved Son, Our Lord, Jesus Christ, in atonement for our sins and those of the whole world."

On the small beads we pray:

"For the sake of His sorrowful Passion, have mercy on us and the whole world."

And at the end, we pray three times:

"Holy God, Holy Mighty One, Holy Immortal One, have mercy on us and on the whole world" (*Diary*, 476).

The Feast of The Divine Mercy

Our Lord asked Blessed Faustina to pray and work toward establishing a Feast of The Divine Mercy on the Sunday after Easter. He told her:

"On that day the very depths of My tender mercy are open. I pour out a whole ocean of graces upon those souls who approach the fount of My mercy. The soul that will go to Confession and receive Holy Communion shall obtain complete forgiveness of sins and punishment" (*Diary*, 699).

It is a day that would celebrate the paschal mystery with a focus on God's covenant of mercy. It would be a day of complete forgiveness and pardon, like the day of atonement in the Old Testament (see Leviticus 16) — all our sins and the punishment due to them would be atoned for.

We can already celebrate this "Mercy Sunday" by going to Confession (preferably before that Sunday) and by receiving Communion on that day. We can honor the mercy of the Lord by our prayers and works of mercy.

The Novena Before the Feast

In preparation for the Feast of The Divine Mercy, the Lord asked Blessed Faustina to make a novena of prayer from Good Friday to the following Saturday.

These nine days of prayer (the word "novena" means nine) before the Feast of Mercy are like the nine days of prayer in the upper room before the day of Pentecost (see Acts 1:14).

For each of the nine days, our Lord gave Blessed Faustina a different intention: all mankind, especially sinners; the souls of priests and religious; all devout and faithful souls; those who do not believe in God and those who do not yet know Jesus; the souls of those who have separated themselves from the Church; the meek and humble souls and souls of little children; the souls who especially venerate and glorify His mercy; the souls detained in purgatory; and souls who have become lukewarm.

"I desire that during these nine days you bring souls to the fount of My mercy, that they may draw therefrom strength and refreshment and whatever graces they have need of in the hardships of life and, especially, at the hour of death" (*Diary*, 1209).

We, too, can make a novena of prayer for these intentions and others, especially by praying the Chaplet of Divine Mercy.

The Three O'clock Hour

In His revelations to Blessed Faustina, Jesus asked for special, daily remembrance at three o'clock, the very hour He died for us on the cross:

"At three o'clock, implore My mercy, especially for sinners; and, if only for a brief moment, immerse yourself in My Passion, particularly in My abandonment at the moment of agony. This is the hour of great mercy for the whole world. I will allow you to enter into My mortal sorrow. In this hour, I will refuse nothing to the soul that makes a request of Me in virtue of My Passion" (*Diary*, 1320).

At three o'clock we can pray:

"You expired, Jesus, but the source of life gushed forth for souls, and the ocean of mercy opened up for the whole world. O Fount of Life, unfathomable Divine Mercy, envelop the whole world and empty Yourself out upon us" (*Diary*, 1319).

"O Blood and Water, which gushed forth from the Heart of Jesus as a fount of mercy for us, I trust in You" (*Diary*, 84).

Spiritual Life of Blessed Faustina

The spiritual life of Blessed Faustina was based on her humility and her obedience to the will of God. On this foundation the structure of her spiritual life was formed — devotion to the Eucharist, Confession, Mary, Suffering, and Intercession.

Peace

The only source of peace in our troubled world is the mercy of God. The Lord made it clear to us through Blessed Faustina:

"Mankind will not have peace until it turns with trust to my mercy!" (*Diary*, 300).

The essence of the Divine Mercy message and devotion is to *trust* in His mercy and *be merciful* to others.

In the words given to Blessed Faustina:

"Jesus, I trust in You!" (*Diary*, 327).

In the words of Jesus in the Gospel:

"Be merciful, even as your Father is merciful" (Lk 6:36 RSV).

(The Marian Helpers Center has developed extensive material that expands on this message of Divine Mercy, including the videocassette and 16 mm film of the motion picture "Divine Mercy — No Escape," as well as books, pamphlets, and reproductions of the Sacred Image of The Divine Mercy. All these and others are available from: Marians of the Immaculate Conception, Marian Helpers, Stockbridge, MA 01263; 1-800-462-7426 U.S.A.; 1-800-344-2836 Canada; © 1993 Marian Helpers.)

Hypatia Tarleton

And a little child shall lead them

I was raised in Lovettsville, a small town in northern Virginia, just a few miles south of the Potomac River, which divides Virginia from Maryland. Our family consisted of my parents, Dick (Richard, Sr.) and Nancy Mullen, and my younger brother, Richard. Until I was a teenager, our family attended church every Sunday.

When I turned eighteen I married Chad Fox, although my parents did not approve of him. At about this time I stopped attending church. Heather Hypatia Fox, our little girl, was born September 18, 1974. Chad abused me mentally and physically for seven years, until we separated and then divorced.

Frank and Doris Tarleton lived in Baltimore, where they raised four sons and a daughter before moving to Brunswick. Their son Mark also went to church every Sunday with his family, and also stopped attending in his late teens.

I met Mark Tarleton while both of us were working for the Railroad Car Yard in Brunswick in June, 1980. Mark was a burner, while I was a welder. For the next five years we dated, still neither of us attending church. Then we married, and for the next five years we still did not attend church.

When we were planning to marry, Mark and I inquired about getting married in the Catholic Church, since both of our families are Catholic. We had already picked the date of June 29, 1985, for the wedding, so when Father Hiltz said that we could not be married unless my first marriage was declared null, we went to the Lutheran minister, Mr. Kretsinger, who married us in the Lutheran Church. Father Hiltz said that Mark and I would be living in sin unless my marriage to Chad was annulled. A little over a year after marrying Mark, our son, Preston Allen Tarleton, was born on July 8, 1986.

When Preston was four months old, we asked Father Hiltz to baptize our baby, but he refused because we were not attending church. My parents, who were deeply offended by Father Hiltz's decision, also stopped going to church. Thank God, they came back later!

When Preston was sixteen months old he had a fever of one-hundred-three degrees, so I put him in a cool bath until his temperature dropped, and Mark and I took turns holding him bundled in blankets. Later we discovered that this had been a mistake, that all clothing should be removed from a child with a fever. Later that evening, while I was preparing dinner and Mark was holding Preston, our baby started to go into seizures.

My God! What a nightmare to see that little body kicking and thrusting, trembling all over. While Mark breathed life into Preston, I called 911. The ambulance took Preston to the Leesburg, Virginia, hospital, where they did a spinal tap and several tests. During the four hours that we were in the Leesburg Hospital, Preston was unconscious. The doctor in Leesburg suggested that we take Preston to Children's Hospital in Washington, D.C.

Preston was at Children's Hospital for five days. I stayed

with him, almost going stir crazy, but the time was not without humorous episodes. Everything at Children's Hospital has been designed for small folk, so since I even took my showers in his room, I had to do so on my knees — until the last night, when I complained to Mark, who simply took off the nozzle and moved it up higher. Even now the family teases me about the little shower!

While he was at Children's Hospital, Preston had several seizures. Tests were run. When he was released, the doctors told us that Preston could have seizures at any time, although he might outgrow them. The whole family prayed for Preston's recovery, and even though I was not going to church, I prayed constantly for him. He has never had another seizure.

In March, 1991, Preston had a cough with a fever for a few days. So I took him to our family physician, who said that he wanted to see Preston again if the fever continued for another couple of days. Shortly after that, Preston's condition worsened quickly. He was unable to eat, had chills, and complained that it hurt to lie on one side. Since our family physician was not available when I called, I took Preston to another Brunswick physician, who said our child had pneumonia. I broke down crying to think that he would have to spend more time in a hospital, this time Frederick Memorial.

As soon as we arrived at the hospital, a therapist started clapping on Preston's lungs to try to break up the congestion that was hindering his breathing. The poor child required oxygen, antibiotics, and intravenous feeding for a week.

In all of the churches in Brunswick and nearby, people were praying for Preston. We told Preston about this every day. That prayer support greatly helped and encouraged us as well as him.

A week later on March 30, when we thought Preston could be released to go home, his doctor ordered X-rays. I could see that the doctor was pale as I walked toward him to hear the results. Further tests would be necessary because Preston had a shadow over one lung. First we would have to sign papers giving permission to take fluid from Preston's lung, because the procedure entailed the danger that the lung might collapse.

Mark stayed in Preston's room to hold our little boy while the doctor inserted a (to us) huge needle into Preston's back. The yellow-tinged fluid that was drawn indicated infection, so a different doctor came, gave Preston a shot of novocaine, and almost immediately made two inch-long cuts into Preston's chest, into which he inserted tubes. Mark told me that as the doctor inserted the tubes into Preston's chest, infectious fluid shot across the room. Then the child was hooked up to a pleurivac.

Mark was so frightened by this experience and the fear that he had seen in Preston's eyes that the next day he visited Father Hiltz. Mark and I believed that it was time for us to return to church, and that what was happening was a test of the sincerity of our prayers. Father Hiltz started the work on the possibility of having my first marriage declared null.

Before Preston's illness, Mark and I had never dwelt much on the subject of attending Mass on Sundays. We had been raised by good families, with basically Catholic Christian beliefs and decent morals, but we did not even talk about the fact that we were not going to church.

When Preston had to undergo the procedure to release the fluid in his lungs we prayed deeply and long. We begged God to let our little boy pull through this ordeal. We knew that we needed God in our lives.

That morning, after the intubation of Preston's chest and the connection to the pleurivac, Preston was transferred to Children's Hospital in Washington, D.C. After a week there, the doctors questioned whether the tubes in his chest were positioned properly. So Preston was brought to a small room to check on that. Neither Mark nor I could be present for this procedure.

Preston was still receiving antibiotics, and still getting intravenous fluids. After nineteen days in Children's Hospital, we were told that because fluid was beginning to collect outside the lung, and pressure was causing his heart and spinal cord to shift, Preston would need an operation. The anesthesiologist came to Preston's room the next morning to give him a preliminary medication through the IV to make him sleepy. As it began to take effect, Preston asked me why I was crying. I told him that I was just a little sad because he had been sick for so long.

The operation was successful! He had become so used to being in hospitals that when a nurse or technician would come to take blood, Preston would raise his arm for the procedure without being asked.

Finally it was time for him to leave the hospital. Three days later, our thirty-eight-pound little boy came home. He looked like one of the starving children in the refugee camps whose pictures we see in newspapers. As we drove up to the house, we were greeted by clusters of balloons on the porch and other decorations arranged by Preston's aunt, my brother's wife.

Preston needed physical therapy to learn how to walk again, but thanks to God, Preston has been healthy ever since.

About a year later, in August, 1992, my first marriage was declared null, so Mark and I could be married in the Church.

We live each day a little better now that we have God back in our lives. Prayer makes us a stronger and more loving family. Mark and I have become very close since we have been attending Mass regularly. There is so much I need to learn, and often after Sunday Mass I find that I have learned something new.

Before this time of terrible trouble I never really thought about just sitting and saying the Our Father or a Hail Mary. Now I find myself blessing my children before they go to bed and asking their guardian angels to look after them.

Our parents are happy that we found our way back to Church. I think of us before Preston's illness as "lost kids." God helped us in our time of need and brought us home. This experience is still new to us, but after Communion it feels good to leave the

Church knowing how we came back and knowing that God answered our prayers even though we had not been going to Church for years. This is truly Divine Mercy. God really does listen to us all.

Dorothy Olszewski

Dottie talks

Life was simple for anyone who was born into a Polish family, living in a Polish neighborhood. My parents, brother, sister, and I shared a second-floor apartment in my grandmother's house in Fells Point, Baltimore. Families were important in those days before World War II. The members of the family did almost everything together, whether it was meals around a table, sharing the stories of what happened at work and at school, or shopping with father, mother, and children doing most of their shopping together, or holiday excursions, again all together.

Living with Busia (Grandmother) was wonderful, because no one loved me as she did. That good, hardworking, spiritual person taught me the things which became the groundwork for the rest of my life. I was in Busia's kitchen more than my parents'. Her kitchen was always warm and full of the homey smells of chicken soup and apples baking. We took turns in Busia's comfortable rocker. I still love to rock. Above all, there was Busia, who could make anyone feel as if he or she were the best person in the world.

When I was nine years old, the second floor apartment was no longer large enough for our family, so we moved to the country, where my father's family lived. I felt my life could never be the same. Not only did I have to attend a public school instead of the Catholic school in our Polish parish, but now I could see Busia only once a week, on Saturdays when we went to town.

Visits to town were always *good*. I remember how delicious our lunch was, with fresh ham and cheese from the corner grocery store accompanied by those special "two-cent pickles." A bakery nearby baked bread all day long, so the bread was always fresh, still warm. Dessert was always something special from that same Polish bakery. Busia never made coffee, so we drank tea — hot in the winter, iced in the summer.

Since there were no stores near our home in the country, we shopped just once a week, on our Saturday visit to town. Even a hole worn in the sole of a shoe had to be repaired by stuffing a piece of cardboard inside until the following Saturday. After an intense round of shopping, back to Busia's for laughter and sharing of stories of the events of the week. Sometimes relatives who lived nearby would drop in for a visit. Children and young teenagers did not wander far from home. Parents knew where their children were at all times; at least mine did. My childhood was a cozy time.

My teen years were routine: go to school, do household chores, go to Church every Sunday with my family. Young teenage girls did not have boyfriends.

I graduated from high school while World War II was still raging, with everyone asked to help with the war effort. So I went to work in the payroll department at Western Electric, which later became AT&T. In the company as I knew it, the employees were treated as one big family. There I met Victoria Panceszyn (now Victoria Elieson), who became my best friend. Her family treated me as one of them. I called her mother "Mom Number Two" and her father "Pop Number Two." I felt rich having a second set of parents like my own, hardworking, down-to-earth people.

Since I had been brought up to love hard, honest work, working hard at Western Electric was easy for me. My single life comprised work, fun, work, fun, work, fun. Then I decided to go to college at night school and my life turned into study, work, fun, study, work, fun. . . . This changed when the hard work paid off as I became the first female supervisor, long before women's lib became popular.

Becoming one of the boys in management required more, and special, studies so that I could become more effective on the job, and also required travel. I enjoyed shopping for clothes, wearing fashionable clothes, playing as hard as I worked. I was under pressure, but I loved it and I enjoyed being around men most of the time. Most of the men were pleasant, charming, interesting, but something seemed to be missing, so I never developed a lasting relationship with any one man.

Dancing was one of my favorite recreations, so I spent a lot of time in cocktail lounges. One night I led a conga line around a bar, between tables, on the bar, having so much fun that the line would not let me stop. I was known in the family as "swinging Aunt Dot." If there is anything to the expression, "Let a smile be your umbrella," I never got wet, because I was always smiling.

I was working hard and letting the good times roll, too busy to look within. I went to church, kept the commandments, was never what most people would call "bad." There seemed to be no need to worry about where I was going.

Being successful at my job enabled me to take early retirement. Then life started to change. Every day began with Mass. New friends met at church invited me to join a prayer group. I found that I wanted to know more about Jesus. But living the good life still took up large amounts of my time.

Gradually, almost imperceptibly, my ideas changed about what made a good time. As most of my new friends invited me,

I found myself attending more prayer meetings and devotions. Since these changes were filling me with joy, I thirsted to know more about Jesus.

One day a friend invited me to a meeting of the Divine Mercy Committee, telling me, "You would be good for them." I backed off, afraid that it would be just a group of women using a committee meeting as an excuse for a social evening, much conversation, and not much accomplished. She kept pressing, so that finally I gave in just to end the pressure.

The meeting was the exact opposite of what I had feared. Although nothing exciting happened, the group was friendly and interesting and their work full of potential for good. So I attended a second and then a third meeting. Then I was asked to be a lector at the annual Celebration of Mercy Sunday, the Sunday following Easter, at Baltimore's Cathedral of Mary, Our Queen.

The day arrived. I was all dressed up. Before Mass, a beautiful stained-glass window in the sacristy depicting Jesus hanging on the cross drew my attention. I mentioned it to Marge Connor, founder of the Divine Mercy Committee of the Archdiocese of Baltimore. Pointing to the crucifix depicted in the window, she responded, "That's what Divine Mercy is all about."

I did the assigned reading. Then, as I knelt again in the sacristy during the Celebration, the window seemed to come alive as thought after thought passed through my mind and heart as if Jesus were talking to me. I began to realize how much Jesus loved me and the whole world. He suffered and died to save me and the whole world. Now He was asking me to help Him to do this. I asked, "How?" The answer was, "Spread My Mercy to the whole world." After Communion, Jesus seemed as close as if He were holding me. Then I seemed to hear, "Get back to your heritage. You are to lector at Holy Rosary Church next Mercy Sunday."

As I shared this almost incredible experience with Marge Connor, our chairwoman, after Mass, we looked at each other and smiled, almost laughed. But that was not the end. Thoughts kept coming — coming — coming: thoughts about how to make the work of the Divine Mercy committee more effective, how to spread the message to more people.

Finally I went to Holy Rosary Church to talk with the pastor, Father Ron Pytel. After I related what had happened, instead of laughing at me, he and I started to plan a celebration for Holy Rosary Church for the next Mercy Sunday. On that Sunday, I was back to my Polish heritage as a returned parishioner and lector. After Communion that Sunday, again I felt held by Jesus, but now the message seemed to be, "Build My Divine Mercy Shrine here at Holy Rosary."

I mentioned that message to Father Ron, though I did nothing for months. Then one day as I was sitting in my favorite rocker I kept having the same thought — "Dedicate My Divine Mercy Shrine on October 5." I wondered what could be significant about October 5, then looked at the magazine next to me. There was an article relating that Blessed Faustina's first Feast Day would be October 5, the anniversary of her death. She had been declared "Blessed" on Mercy Sunday by Pope John Paul II, the Sunday Jesus had seemed to say, "Build My Shrine."

October 5 was only seven weeks away! Margie and the Committee members hurried to plans to bring the Shrine to completion in this short time, despite the fact that for every advance there was a set-back. When October 5 came, the Divine Mercy Shrine was ready and Holy Rosary Church was filled with devoted people from all over the archdiocese. The dedication ceremonies started early in the afternoon and ended with Mass celebrated by Bishop John Ricard, the spiritual director and moderator of the Divine Mercy Committee.

Even my Busia was at the Dedication! At the reception which followed the Mass, a cousin handed me a package. While I was wondering what the gift could be, he asked, "Do you remember this?" "This" was a picture which had been in Busia's home many years ago, a copy of the first Divine Mercy image painted

according to Blessed Faustina's directions. What a confirma-
tion of Busia's teachings to me in my young girlhood! That
very special image now hangs in my home.

If we had any thoughts about slowing down, they were soon
dispersed. The work had to grow, because it is Jesus' work, not
ours. My friend Vicki wanted to help, so she furthered her com-
puter knowledge with additional classes, and is now our secretary and is developing various publications including the Divine Mercy quarterly newsletter, brochures, and ads. I never
realized how much my life had become centered around Jesus'
Mercy until one day someone mentioned "Levis" to me and I
thought she was speaking of Jesus' tax collector disciple before
I realized she was talking about blue jeans!

Has my outlook on the world become narrowed? Have I lost
my *joie de vivre*, my capacity for fun? Of course not! Actually
my joy in living springs from a deeper source, commitment to
and acceptance of God's will, so no apparent set-backs can
destroy that happiness. Accepting His will becomes easier and
easier, and the fun bubbles up because around every next corner is God, nothing to fear.

Marge O'Connor

God's mercy through His holy priests

As I began to write about my spiritual pilgrimage, it became difficult to separate my spiritual pilgrimage from the story of my entire life of fifty-nine years. The task seemed overwhelming. Then, while I was on retreat this year, it seemed as if the Holy Spirit moved me to focus on God's priests and their role in my life, as teachers, counselors, confessors, friends, and most of all on Jesus.

First there was Father McLane, of St. Andrew's Parish in Drexel Hill, Pennsylvania, who baptized me. Then Father Clair Hammill, associate pastor at Good Shepherd Parish in southwest Philadelphia, who impressed me so much when I was three by borrowing one of the boys' bikes to give me a ride on the handlebars! He would go fishing with my father and some of the other men of the parish, meeting in our kitchen for breakfast in the middle of the night, because my mother was the only wife who would get up early enough to allow them to reach the fishing grounds while the fish were biting.

In those days, people went to confession frequently and lines for confessions were long, except at Father Hammill's confessional. Perhaps people felt intimidated by him. But not Margie! I would even start my confession by saying, "Bless me Father, for I have sinned. This is Margie." His sound advice has proved useful many times through the years.

My big brother Bill entrusted me with his very first new car while he did Navy Reserve time. I was twenty-two years old and right out of nurse's training and ready to take care of the world. Driving home from Mass on Easter Sunday, I totaled Bill's car and nearly totaled myself, with a fractured skull and jaw, and was in a coma for a week. When I saw blood coming from my right ear, I knew I was in trouble, but reasoned that I could not die then because nurses were so needed. After I awakened from the coma, surgeons repaired my upper jaw and placed a little box on my right cheek which read "Do not touch."

I really wondered and worried about how Bill would react to what I had done to his precious car. How far does family love stretch? But after Bill returned from his reserve time, he visited me in the hospital, kissed my swollen face, and greeted me with "Hi kid!" That was real Christ-like mercy.

At that time, Dad was still mourning Mom's death from three years before, and also suffering from the loss of his coal business. My eldest sister, Ann, had left home to become an airline stewardess. Bill was living at home after four years of life as a naval officer, but in straitened circumstances because he was busy studying to complete his degree. Mary Jane, next to me in age, had just become engaged, and was trying unsuccessfully to manage our family finances. Without insurance coverage, my medical bills were huge.

In this family crisis, I turned to Father Hammill. He advised me to leave home! I could not believe my ears! "What about my Dad?" Father Hammill told me, "Ask if he minds that you leave, and even if he does, leave anyway." Dad told me to do as Father Hammill had advised.

I stayed with some friends who were also nurses and left the problems behind. Just one week later, Mary Jane asked me to come home to cook dinner for Dad and Bill since she had other plans for that evening. I did so, and was treated like a queen. The next day we had an impromptu family conference around the kitchen table after dinner, the same kitchen table where we had so often prayed the Rosary with Mom.

Each of us poured out our feelings, especially about each other. It was done with compassion and love. What a catharsis! Resolutions were made, and I moved back home that night for a new start.

Father Hammill went to eternity in 1966 after suffering from emphysema for several years. He had been a special "other Christ" to me for many years. Now I believe he continues to pray for me in the presence of God.

Looking back, it seems as though there were several years when I had little contact with priests other than Mass and occasional confession, although one episode comes to mind. I remember, as a young head nurse at Hahnemann Hospital, staying all night with a dying priest after working the full day shift. What a privilege! But generally, I was busy as a hospital supervisor, and after work learning to ski, partying, and looking for someone great to marry. I still lived at home with Dad. My sisters had married, and my brother was traveling the world as an airline pilot.

In 1973, when I was thirty-eight, an opportunity came to study at Johns Hopkins to become a new kind of nurse, a pediatric nurse-practitioner. It would be a more independent role for a nurse. I loved doing what only doctors had done heretofore. Pride often kept me from admitting my shortcomings. Relying more on myself than on the Divine Physician causes anxiety.

After Dad died in 1975 following four years of cancer, I felt more free, ready to sell the family home of the past forty years, ready to move anywhere. A nurse-practitioner position was offered in Baltimore, so I moved in January, 1977. Adjustment was easy, learning to like soft crabs and beer and joining a tennis circuit. I felt in "great shape" and that all was well: a Class A tennis player with a good job, driving a 280 Z sports car, and occasionally dating a good-looking single man. I joined a rather new Catholic Church near my home in Baltimore County, and through a Renew Program met Catholic friends.

A retired couple, Joe and Kathleen Walter, members of a charismatic prayer group, watched with loving concern while I became involved with the New Age movement at the same time. Before leaving Philadelphia, I had learned hypnosis, taught by a nurse from a Catholic hospital. I now had the opportunity to include hypnosis for children with some chronic problems in my practice. In Baltimore, I began to study macrobiotics with its pantheistic philosophy.

In October, 1991, a slipped lumbar disc literally knocked me off my feet. After a week, an orthopedic surgeon said that all he could do was to "sever a nerve." I chose to spend the next three weeks in bed. At the end of each week I would attempt to get up and function, but with no success. All this time for myself brought questions.

It was a switch for me to think about myself and my feelings, and it was strange to think that I might need some care after twenty years of caring for others. I searched the house for something to read and found *The Road Less Traveled* by Scott Peck. Not a Catholic book, it contains some elements of New Age, and although parts could have applied to me, I found myself tending to relate those parts to others. I began to pray the Rosary again and rested well.

A new friend and neighbor, Gwen Nicholson, visited daily, brought food, and listened and listened as I vented. We have remained close friends. Again, God's mercy. Kathleen Walter visited with soup and brought a cassette tape of Sister Briege McKenna, whose ministry is to priests and about the Eucharist. I cannot recall the message of that first tape, but it touched me.

After four weeks without improvement, I made an appointment with a neurosurgeon. The day before my appointment with him, Kathleen called at 4 p.m. to tell me about a nun, Sister Beatrice Novotny, SSND, whom she had read about in our local newspaper. Sister Beatrice, in her 80s, was "retired" but involved in an active healing ministry, and could be called between 3:30 and 4:30 p.m. I was sufficiently desperate to call immediately.

Sister Beatrice asked me three questions: Did I watch "the soaps"? I did not. Did I read the daily horoscope? Yes. Did I have any anger or resentment against anyone? Immediately I thought of my sister, Mary Jane, and my brother. I was unaware of the feelings until now.

As I sobbed and sobbed, Sister Bea told me that God had forgiven me and that I was to cast my anger into the sea as she quoted Scripture. Then she sang. The tears I cried that night accompanied healing.

The next morning as I prepared to keep my appointment with the neurosurgeon I felt no pain and discovered that I could move freely. When my sister Ann arrived from Harrisburg to take me to the doctor, I told her the story of my conversation with Sister Bea. The doctor took my medical history, including the sudden relief from pain I had just experienced. After he completed what I thought was a normal neurological examination, he informed me that I had a slipped disc which was getting better.

In spite of this diagnosis, the neurosurgeon ordered a back brace and another week of bed rest. After just one more day in bed I lost all patience (not my best gift) and asked my sister to bring me to her home. This required me to travel there lying in her station wagon. Four normal teens and a dog contributed nothing toward my recovery. So I returned home, bent like a pretzel and wearing the nuisance of a brace.

A variety of treatments followed — physical therapy, chiro-
practors, yoga, movement exercises, macrobiotic food, and daily
swimming laps, all while I tried to resume my normal work and
social life. During those years there was a spiritual void in my
life, but because there was no priest to point it out I failed to
recognize it.

After Sister Beatrice's death, Father Larry Gesy took over
her ministry of healing. My back seemed to be improving slowly
as I attended a few of his healing services. After a while we
shared accounts of some of the Eastern, New Age practices in
which he had been and I was involved.

Joe and Kathleen were gently nudging me to join their charismatic prayer group, to take a "Life in the Spirit" course. I was
too busy for that until Linda Gianneccini, a friend who lived in
the same parish whom I had met in a macrobiotic cooking class,
gave me a book to read "right away." Before I had completed
half of Constance Cumbey's *The Hidden Dangers of the Rain-
bow*, I called Kathleen to insist that she get me into the "Life in
the Spirit" seminar immediately, even though the course had
already begun. She did. With the counsel and advice of Father
Larry, I abandoned my New Age beliefs and practices and sought
God's forgiveness for having followed this new fad.

The seminar was just what I needed, and I was ready for it.
For about a year I cried at every meeting. Some of those present
informed me that I had "the gift of tears." Whether or not, the
crying relieved my tension (or was the result of my release of
the tension) and often made me look like a panda from running
mascara!

In December, 1984, I felt a need to make a retreat to prepare
for Christmas (the last time I had made a retreat had been in
high school). During the retreat, Father Ed Winchman showed
a video about Mejugorie. Watching it again, I knew that I had
to go there soon, although when I finally went in October, 1986,
I thought that I would be very bored with nothing to do but pray
all day. On the contrary, by the third day, my fellow-pilgrims

almost had to drag me out of the church at 8 p.m. to catch the bus to our hotel. Our spiritual director for that trip was Father Jack Collopy. It was nice to discover that he was from the neighborhood in which I had lived as a child and to share stories.

On our first day in Medjugorje, just after we arrived in the parking lot about 4 p.m., someone said, "Margie, come look at the sun." Looking up, I saw at first a light gray disc over the sun. Then it appeared to be within a shimmering gold monstrance, with bright pastel colors coming from it. Beside it was a gold chalice. We began to sing spontaneously, "O Sacrament Most Holy, O Sacrament Divine. . . ." We were laughing and crying with joy.

The following day the same thing occurred. It could easily become routine. Just as we take for granted God's beautiful gifts of sunrise and sunset and all the rest of creation, mountains, oceans, plants . . . so even the Holy Eucharist can be taken for granted, become routine.

One very chilly evening, after dark, a few of us were still standing in front of the church. A young woman, wrapped in an old army blanket, was sitting up against the front wall of the Church. I pulled out a five-dollar bill, approached her, and said, "I thought you could use this." She took it, smiled, and said "Thank you." As I turned to leave, I saw extending from the blanket two little legs, with high brown shoes and no socks. Back again with my friends, I thought, "Here you are, a pediatric nurse, and you didn't even ask about her little child! He could have been sick!" I tried to find the woman, but she had gone.

I returned to the church, and to the "apparition room," which was seldom unlocked for visitors. In that room is a statue of our Lady, the face of which is not at all pretty, even rather ugly, which moved me to say to the Blessed Mother in my prayer, "When will I see how you *really* look?" I clearly "heard in my heart" rather than audibly, "You just saw me outside." Again, I cried for joy.

After two years in the charismatic prayer group, I was led to a parish Bible study group. Here I learned how to use the Bible and to love the Scriptures. At about this time, some of my friends and I started a Marian group at the Cathedral of Mary Our Queen.

Both of my sisters joined us on another Medjugorje trip, and more family healing occurred there between us. Healing often seems to take place a bit at a time, over and over, in "layers," and often the right time and place for healing indicates that His Mother has been interceding for us.

In 1989, St. Francis Xavier, an inner-city church, became my place to attend daily Mass because it was close to my work. Weekday Masses were offered in the rectory chapel. The first time I went there for weekday Mass, I was unable to find the rectory door behind the church so I was late. After I rang the doorbell, a vested priest greeted me at the door and led me into the small chapel where I discovered he had been in the middle of Mass. As I looked around, I thought, "This is a holy place," then, "What a holy priest!"

After Mass, the priest chatted with me for a moment then left. The only other person present was a little old lady named Flossie, so I asked her the name of the priest. She looked at me with surprise and said, "Why, that's Bishop Ricard!"

When I returned for Mass the next day, Bishop Ricard pointed to the Lectionary and said, "Read." I responded, "I don't do that." He repeated, "Read." So I read . . . and still read.

Bishop Ricard was very tolerant of my excitement about my trips to Medjugorje and the "birthday parties" in my home to celebrate the Feast of the Nativity (or "birthday") of Our Lady. He had to have been amused by one of the pictures which showed the Pilgrim Statue of Our Lady of Fatima from an angle where it appeared as if she were blowing out the candles on her cake.

On another trip to Medjugorje, someone gave me a copy of a Novena to the Divine Mercy a few days before Mercy Sunday. The next year I ordered a hundred copies of that novena. I took the Divine Mercy Novena leaflets to St. Francis Church and asked the pastor, Father John Filipelli, if we might pray the Novena after daily Mass before Mercy Sunday. He agreed to that and handed me a package from Bishop Ricard. In the package was a video about Blessed Faustina, her diary, a biography, and another book. A note attached to the package read: "Dear Friend of Our Lady, I thought you'd know what to do with this. From Bishop John Ricard." Coincidence or Providence?

Right after that (and I'm sure providentially) I had foot surgery which required that I be off my feet for three weeks, just enough time to read and meditate on Blessed Faustina's biography.

The following year, 1990, I attended the first Mercy Sunday celebration, in the National Shrine of the Immaculate Conception in Washington, D.C. I thought Baltimore should have the same big celebration. When I presented that idea to Bishop Ricard the next day, as something for him to take care of, his response was, "Put it together." And now? Five years later, we have just had our Fifth Archdiocesan Divine Mercy Celebration in twenty-one different places in Maryland, with thousands attending. Baltimore also has a Divine Mercy Shrine at beautiful Holy Rosary Church, and a pilgrimage to Poland is planned. Bishop Ricard remains very close to us as the spiritual director and moderator of our Divine Mercy Committee which he started after our first celebration.

At the end of one of our monthly sessions, Father Jack Collopy prayed that many priests would be sent to me. At the time, that seemed strange to me, but I continue to meet and work with many holy priests.

Once I was looking for a group of Mother Teresa's associates who met weekly to pray together. I finally found them at the little convent at St. Michael's Overleigh, and there in the convent chapel found Exposition of the Blessed Sacrament. Father Frank Genovese was there for the first time also. He would always face the Blessed Sacrament and begin talking to Jesus.

Almost before we knew it, Father Frank's voice seemed to be Jesus talking to us. In his seventies, Father Frank had suffered from cancer for years, still tall and straight as an arrow, very thin, but mentally sharp, humorous, and full of enthusiasm. As his health failed, I sometimes spent Sunday afternoons with him when he was unable to join his delightful Italian and Polish family outings.

When Father Frank was in the hospital for the last time, I visited him early one morning unaware that he was scheduled to be discharged later that day, "Now what do you want?" he asked. I told him that I was bringing him a Divine Mercy image, and he found a place for it. Later, when his niece Joannie arrived he said, "Guess who came today," and pointed to the image of Jesus. At 3:00 p.m. that same afternoon (July 27, 1992), as he was reciting the Divine Mercy Chaplet with Joannie, Father Frank went home to God.

One of the special religious sisters in my life was Mother Solidad, of the Handmaids of the Sacred Heart. With no musical gifts at all, nevertheless I was taking piano lessons from her, so I would encourage her to talk about Jesus. Then suddenly the bells would chime and the "music lesson" was over. I would have to force her to take the money my parents had given me for the lesson. Once she said she would pray every day for me to have a religious vocation. She said Jesus was the most reliable husband. Sometimes I wonder if I missed that special call. A few years ago, my sister Mary Jane said that she had heard that Mother Solidad was in Spain doing work similar to Mother Teresa's work in Calcutta.

Which brings me to Mother Teresa. My first experience with Mother Teresa was in Philadelphia in the early seventies. I was working in south Philadelphia. On my lunch hour I raced to the Convention Center. Thousands of people were milling around. I went into the hall and sat. Some officials brought a tiny nun in blue and white onto the stage to say a few words. Up I went, reached out, and touched her before she was whisked off. Then I rushed back to work. Later I read that that particular convention was a Charismatic Conference and years later I discovered that the nun I was moved to touch was Mother Teresa.

In 1993, Mother Teresa's Missionaries of Charity opened a house in Baltimore for homeless men dying of AIDS. On a Saturday afternoon when the sisters had been here only a short time, I was produce shopping at a farm near the city. I thought of the sisters and asked the farmer if he had any extra produce. He filled my little car. As I drove into the inner city at four in the afternoon, I asked myself, "What am I doing?" But when I arrived at the convent and asked the sisters if they needed the food, they responded that they had prayed for food the night before.

The "Gift of Hope" house of Mother Teresa's Missionaries of Charity has been a refuge for me. The sisters' joy, holiness, and reverence for the Blessed Sacrament and devotion to Mary, as well as their compassion for these needy men, are greatly moving. Our Divine Mercy Committee volunteers there regularly to clean, to bring meals, to provide transport for the sisters, and to pray with the dying men.

My back continued to improve over the years, but not without episodes of pain and the added insult of another injury from an auto accident. Monthly visits to the chiropractor continued. Then in July, 1993, my insurance coverage for that expense was terminated. During a retreat which I made shortly after that, each day, for three days in a row, one of the retreat leaders "called out a back healing." Each time this happened I thought it was for someone else. Then, with pain still in my neck and sacrum, but nice tingling in mid-back, I thought it might be a gradual healing.

When I related the story to Father Jack, he scolded me for not accepting God's healing. Then he advised me to ask Jesus to cover me with His Blood whenever I might have pain, and to cast out any evil spirits within or around me, and to immediately ask the Holy Spirit to fill me with His gifts. That advice has worked well for me ever since. Later, when I thanked Father Jack he didn't even remember giving me that advice. Praise God for His healing and mercy!

A poem by Father John Bannister Tabb, which was given to me when I was just a small child, has always seemed to sum up God's plan for me:

Life's Weaving

My life is but a weaving
Between my God and me;
I may not choose the colors,
He knows what they should be;
For He can view the pattern
Upon the upper side,
While I can see it only
On this, the under side.

Sometimes He weaveth sorrow,
Which seemeth strange to me;
But I will trust His judgment
And work on faithfully;
Tis He who fills the shuttle,
He knows just what is best;
So I shall weave in earnest
And leave with Him the rest.

At last when life is ended,
With Him I shall abide,
Then I may view the pattern
Upon the upper side;

Then I shall know the reason
Why pain with joy entwined,
Was woven in the fabric
Of life that God designed.

Abbey of Gethsemani, Trappist, Kentucky

Father Ronald P. Pytel

A holy healing

I am pastor of Holy Rosary Church in Baltimore, Maryland. This parish church is the Archdiocesan Shrine for Divine Mercy, dedicated on the first Feast Day of Blessed Faustina by Most Reverend John H. Ricard, our auxiliary bishop. When Pope John Paul II visited the United States as Cardinal Karol Wojtyla, he visited and prayed in Holy Rosary Church.

I am of Polish ethnic background. My parents were born in America, but my grandparents came from Poland. Holy Rosary is my home parish where I went to school and was ordained in May, 1973.

The Felician Sisters taught at Holy Rosary School. I remember that when I was a young boy, I had seen in our school the image of Divine Mercy with the inscription *Jezu, ufam Tobie*. I don't remember seeing the image in school later during the period when the devotion was banned. As an adult, I became very well acquainted with the devotion to Divine Mercy and to the chaplet while I was on pilgrimage to Medjugorje in the late 1980s.

Here in the Archdiocese of Baltimore, the Divine Mercy devotions and Mercy Sunday were fostered by Bishop John Ricard at the Cathedral of Mary Our Queen. As the devotion grew, Holy Rosary became the second site for Mercy Sunday. The first Mercy Sunday Celebration was held at Holy Rosary on the day of Blessed Faustina's beatification. On her first feast day, a permanent shrine was blessed at Holy Rosary at the place where Cardinal Wojtyla, now Pope John Paul II, had knelt to pray.

Throughout the spring of 1995 I suffered from what seemed to be a severe allergy. Since I had suffered from hay fever in previous years, I simply took allergy relief medication. Even though it appeared that I was suffering more than before, other people also were suffering more from their allergies because the pollen count was extremely high in Baltimore last spring.

Eventually I thought that I had developed bronchitis, since I found great difficulty breathing when I walked up stairs and I was constantly coughing. A local general medical doctor confirmed that I was suffering from allergic bronchitis, but he also said that a heart murmur that I had had from boyhood seemed more severe, so he made an appointment for me to have a Doppler echocardiagram.

When the echocardiagram was done on June 7, 1995, it showed that my aortic valve was stenotic, that I had only about twenty-five percent blood flow through the valve, and that some blood was "backwashing." In short, I was in cardiac failure. On June 8, Dr. Nicholas Fortuin of Johns Hopkins Hospital, one of the most respected cardiologists in the nation, confirmed that diagnosis of stenosis of the aortic valve after reading the echogram. He prescribed medication and complete bed rest while arranging for surgery at Johns Hopkins Hospital.

Dr. Fortuin arranged for heart catherization on June 12 to ascertain if any arteries leading to the heart were clogged. The catheterization showed my arteries to be clear. As I was recovering from that, Dr. Peter Green, who was scheduled to perform the surgery, informed me that my surgery, originally scheduled for June 13, would be postponed until the fourteenth because an emergency surgery would take precedence since my condition had been stabilized.

On Tuesday, when I reported to the outpatient building for more tests and X-rays, Dr. Green said that I had two options for the replacement valve: 1) a mechanical valve, called the "St. Jude Valve;" or 2) a tissue valve from a pig or a sheep. A tissue valve had a life-span of ten to twelve years and then would require replacement surgery, while the mechanical valve could be expected to last indefinitely, although I would need to take blood thinners for the rest of my life to prevent the clots which might be caused from the metal of which the valve is made.

My parents had been told they would never have children, but my mother prayed to St. Jude and made many novenas, because they desperately wanted children. My mother finally found a doctor who discovered her irregular fertility cycle. After thirteen years of marriage, I was born. My brother was born four years later. Since my mother was so devoted to St. Jude I knew the mechanical valve, the "St. Jude Valve," was my option. The remaining tests were done on June 13.

On the morning of June 14, my best priest friend, Father Larry Gesy, took me to Johns Hopkins Hospital at 6:30 a.m. On the way there Father Larry said to me, "Don't worry, Ron; this is all about Divine Mercy." As a consequence of postponing my surgery for that one day, my heart surgery took place on the first day of the novena before the Feast of the Sacred Heart. Even though I didn't like the prospect of heart surgery, I was at peace.

Surgery was done on the morning of June 14. I was in the intensive care section until the following day. "Step-down" care was filled, so, after the respirator and stomach drainage tubes were removed, the doctor felt that since I was progressing so well, it was safe to move me into a regular room on the cardiac floor of the hospital. The nurses had me up and walking on Thursday afternoon.

Among the things I had packed to bring to the hospital was

the diary of Blessed Faustina. During recovery I read the diary whenever possible, and prayed the chaplet every day.

After the surgery, Dr. Peter Green met with Father Larry, and told him since the valve which had been replaced was so stenotic, the left ventricle was pushing the blood that should have been going through the valve. As a result, the left ventricle was seriously enlarged. Dr. Jacek Mostwin, a urology surgeon at Hopkins and a person friend of Father Larry and myself, was in the operating room during my surgery. After the surgery was completed, Dr. Mostwin told Father Larry that the surgery had gone well, but that my heart had been worked to the maximum and had I waited another month, surgery would have been useless.

Shortly after leaving the hospital, I developed pleurisy. Even though I should have been in pain, I detected that something was wrong only because I had a fever. When I was readmitted to the hospital on July 7, my left lung had to be drained of a liter of fluid. Antibiotics were administered and I was watched as blood cultures were done to make sure that no infection would reach the heart. When the doctors were sure that I was out of danger and my oral medication was regulated, I was discharged, but I looked like a victim of a concentration camp, partly because my weight had dropped from a normal one hundred sixty-five pounds to one hundred forty-four pounds.

During July and August I gradually regained some weight and strength. After my examination in August, I visited Dr. Fortuin. On the same day, Father Larry Gesy had his regular examination. He had suffered a massive heart attack at the age of twenty-three and had developed pneumonia and pleurisy at that time. His doctors had not expected him to recover. He is now forty-seven years old. When Father Larry discussed my situation with Dr. Fortuin, the doctor said that he did not know what kind of life I would be able to resume, that I was basically uninsurable. The damage to the left ventricle was very serious, because my heart had been pushed to the maximum before the surgery. Congestive heart failure had been masked by allergies and bron chitis. Father Larry shared this information with me gradually on my return home from the examination in the hospital.

Later in August I met with Dr. Green, who wanted to make sure the sternum was healing well. I had regained weight and my color was excellent; strength and energy levels were quite good. So Dr. Green was very pleased with my progress. He suggested that at my scheduled visit with Dr. Fortuin in November another echogram be taken to determine whether the left ventricle showed any sign of strengthening.

During August the Divine Mercy Committee of the Archdiocese of Baltimore went on pilgrimage to Poland to visit the sites of Blessed Faustina's life. Both Father Larry and I had been asked to be chaplains to that pilgrimage and had planned on going. Since my health would not permit it and Father Larry wanted to assist me during the recuperation period, we suggested Father Paul Henry as chaplain. The pilgrimage group prayed for me by name every day at the Masses celebrated at the sites associated with Blessed Faustina's life.

At the tomb of Blessed Faustina in Crack, Miss Dorothy Olszewski, one of my parishioners and co-chairman of the Archdiocesan Committee for Divine Mercy, offered a special prayer. Father Larry had told her of the seriousness of my condition, even before I knew of it. Miss Olszewska told me later that she had spoken from her heart to Blessed Faustina and had asked for a miracle, promising that she would be tireless in her efforts to promote devotion to Divine Mercy and the cause of Blessed Faustina's canonization.

In early September I returned to Holy Rosary Parish to resume my work. After about one week, I stumbled on the stairs one day and injured my left hand, fracturing my little finger and driving a key from the key ring I was holding into the flesh at the base of the thumb. Because I was taking blood thinners, I developed a hematoma that compressed some nerves. This caused loss of sensation in the tip of my thumb and my arm was put in a cast for a week to immobilize the little finger. I had to wear an arm splint for an additional ten days. This occurred while our parish was preparing for the day of prayer and devotions planned for the Feast Day of Blessed Faustina on October 5 in anticipation of the visit of the Holy Father to Baltimore on October 8. The splint was removed just before our celebration of Blessed Faustina's feast day.

On October 5, we celebrated an all-day vigil before the Blessed Sacrament with prayers, the chaplet of Divine Mercy, the Rosary, and talks on our Lord's Gift of Mercy. The day concluded with a concelebrated Mass. Usually Bishop Ricard celebrates the Mass on Blessed Faustina's feast day here at the Archdiocesan Shrine, but because he was in Newark to greet the Holy Father, I was the principal celebrant. In my homily I spoke about trust and about how I believed the Lord was touching me with His mercy. Following the Mass that evening, a group of persons who have a ministry called "Our Father's Work" prayed over me for continued healing, invoking the intercession of Blessed Faustina. Miss Olszewski said later that she felt that Blessed Faustina was really present to us that evening during the Mass and that she was smiling. Later that evening I began to have discomfort in my chest whenever I breathed deeply. This was something new since until this time I had had no chest pain after surgery except from the incision.

The next day, October 6, I called Dr. Fortuin and told him of this new problem and that I believed Zestril, a new medication which he had prescribed, had caused it. Dr. Fortuin suggested that I take a half-dosage every other day or a half-dosage every day, but not to omit it entirely as this was the best possible medication for my heart condition. I tried the half-dosage every day, which relieved the pain.

On November 9, 1995, I once again visited Dr. Fortuin for my scheduled appointment. After an initial examination, a Doppler echocardiagram was taken. Dr. Fortuin viewed the results of the test and then called me into his office. He stared at me silently for what seemed like an eternity. Then he spoke. To the best of my recollection these were his exact words: "Ron, some-one has intervened for you."

"What do you mean?"I asked.

"Your heart is normal," he replied.

"What?" I said.

"Your heart is normal," he repeated.

"Well, Peter Green (the surgeon) had suggested that you do an echocardiagram to see whether the left ventricle was strength-ening," I responded.

"No, no, no. We're saying 'normal.' I was not at all opti-mistic about your condition. I can't explain it," he said.

"A lot of prayer," was my response.

"AND. . . ," he replied.

I said, "Yes, prayer and science."

Dr. Fortuin answered, "Right. You have no restrictions, and I'll see you in a year."

I asked, "A year?" (I felt as if a security blanket had been taken away from me.)

"Yes, a year. Your heart is normal," he said.

Dr. Fortuin reminded me that I must continue to take blood thinners because of having an artificial valve, and that my blood clotting factor must be checked monthly to ensure the correct dosage. He recommended that I continue the half-dosage of Zestril as a precaution. He said that I could discontinue the other medications I'd been taking.

When I phoned Father Larry Gesy after I left Dr. Fortuin's office, Father Larry remarked, "Well, I guess we got the miracle we prayed for."

There was great rejoicing when I shared the news with my pa-rishioners and all those who had been praying for me. I feel fine and have resumed normal activities. I truly believe that God in His mercy has healed me and that Blessed Faustina has interceded for me.

Editor's note: This case is now before the Vatican Congre-gation for the Cause of the Saints as a possible miracle for Blessed Faustina's canonizaiton cause.

Father James McCullough

In the morning let me know Your love

hy me? But then, why not me? Should I be exempt just because I happen to be a priest? Others have cancer. No reason I should be immune.

Cancer! What a truly ugly word! When they apply that term to your own health, it can be truly devastating. Yet, I had to face it; a melanoma near the cones of the interior rear wall of my left eye. There was a very high probability it was encapsulated and wouldn't spread, but certainty would have to wait until the post-operative biopsy. That hope of encapsulation took care of my primary worry. Yet I had a second concern I had voiced to no one, fearing I would appear vain. But it was a very real concern.

The year was 1979. I'd just passed my fifty-first birthday and was approaching my twenty-second anniversary in the priesthood. My entire priestly ministry had been spent teaching and working with young collegians. It had been my life and I dearly loved it. Would this operation, this removal of the eye, interfere with that ministry? I was afraid to ask. Would I be so disfigured it would cause those young people to shy away from me, or somehow make me appear unapproachable? I was concerned.

Monday, May 1, I registered at the Cleveland Clinic. While two priest friends visited with a woman in a wheelchair, I filled out the required forms. Moving to join them I looked more closely at that woman. Her hands shook uncontrollably and her head bobbed from side to side. My guess was multiple sclerosis. The lack of muscular control contorted her attempted smile into a grimace. But her eyes were something else. They radiated warmth and concern as she greeted me: "I just wanted you to know that I'm offering up all I'll have to endure this week so that you'll come through this successfully." Wow! Here I was concerned about the loss of an eye. This poor soul had to spend the rest of her life confined to a wheelchair becoming each day ever more dependent on others, and she was concerned about me! God certainly has a flair for putting things into perspective for me. What a woman! And what a gift when I needed it most.

By Tuesday afternoon, after much testing, the original diagnosis was reaffirmed; the eye would have to be removed. The operation was scheduled for the next morning. That evening I took out my breviary trying to calm my nerves by praying. My mind was in such a turmoil I was just reading words; words without meaning.

Then while reading night prayers I came to Psalm 143. As if leaping out of the page, the words I read were:

> In the morning let me know your love
> for I put my trust in you.
> Make me know the way I should walk:
> to you I lift up my soul (verse 8) (*The Liturgy of*

the Hours, Volume III, Catholic Publishing Company, New York, 1976).

I underlined those words and notated in the book: eye operation; May 3, 1979. I was conscious God was reaching out to draw me toward Him as He had done so often before in my life. I didn't want to forget that moment.

It would be nice to say that after reading those words I then experienced inner peace, but I didn't. I was still very edgy and a bit scared. Unable to sleep later that night, I went down the corridor to have a cigarette in the large room they call the solarium. The room was lighted solely by the outside street light entering through the three glass windows that enclosed the room. The place was empty save for one man sitting with his head buried in his hands. Sensing he'd been given bad news, I pretended to need a light for my cigarette to try to get him talking. He'd been told his cancer had progressed beyond where medicine could help. I said, "I don't know what to say. Are you a praying man?" He answered, "I'd like to think so." I went on, "I'm a Catholic priest. Tomorrow morning they are going to take out my left eye due to a cancer. I need to pray and I'm finding it difficult. Would you mind if we prayed together?"

And so we did. Two total strangers, lonely and scared. We sat facing each other in that semi-dark room, holding each other's hands, tears streaming down our faces, and we prayed as perhaps we had never prayed before. What a powerful moment! Later I would tell my friends that if I could have my eye back but only at the cost of not having had that experience I would not make the trade.

Yet, as powerful as that moment was, there was something else happening during that praying. Clear as a bell I heard an inner voice say, "See, you can still minister." I was startled; but I was also elated. Some might attribute that to some kind of unconscious psychological surfacing of inner fears. Maybe!

But in my heart I know Who it was Who spoke, and I thanked Him.

A day or so later, after the eye had been removed I went again into that solarium. This time I spotted a man off by himself staring blankly out the window. He had cancer of the larynx and they were going to remove his voice box. He told me of his job, his family, and especially of his grown son, whom he obviously loved. He had delayed this operation so that the two of them could take a trip they'd planned. Here I was ministering again, a ministry of just listening and helping him talk. It was a different ministry than before, but it was needed. It confirmed that inner voice for me.

Friday morning I was to be released. Before I left I felt I had to look at that eye and accept its loss. I went into the bathroom, peeled back the bandage and unveiled the socket. Ugly! Black and blue and even purple rings enclosed a socket filled by a clear plastic retainer inserted there to give the eyelid something to ride upon and to keep the lid supple. My stomach turned sour and my knees turned into jelly. I began to sob uncontrollably.

Later I would come to understand I was mourning the loss of the eye. But then I thought I was going into shock. I rang for the nurse to help me get back into my bed. She then called in an aide while she went for a doctor. That aide was another gift from God. A motherly black woman, she held me as if I were an oversized sobbing child. "What's wrong, honey?" she asked. Between sobs I muttered, "I think I'm having a huge case of self-pity." "Go ahead," she said, "you're entitled." Perhaps it was the way she said it, but her words made me chuckle inside and instantly that malevolent mood vanished. I was okay again. The right person at the right time. Coincidence? Or was God still showing me His love?

Eight weeks later, while teaching summer classes, I came to class wearing my new eye, my prothesis. Having worn the eye patch up until then I knew the students would be curious but polite. To spare them furtive staring I told them to take a good look and to ask any questions they wanted to so that we could get beyond all that. They were great, and it went well. Not one seemed to shy away or feel awkward. I was still able to reach them and was approachable for them. The healing was taking place; the fears gone. The cancer was gone; no radiation, no chemotherapy. Just go on with life and be grateful. "In the morning let me know Your love." He did!

(This article originally appeared in the *Newsletter* of the Confraternity of Catholic Clergy, November 1995 issue.)

Catherine Griffin

God of mercy

lessed be the God and Father of our Lord Jesus Christ, the Father of compassion and God of all encouragement, who encourages us in our every affliction, so that we may be able to encourage those who are in any affliction with the encouragement with which we ourselves are encouraged by God (2 Corinthians 1:3, 4).

Sunday, June 18, 1989, was the last time that my husband, Alfred Griffin, and I would attend Mass together at St. Anthony's Church in Falls Church, Virginia. Five months earlier he had been diagnosed with a very rare and invasive form of lung cancer for which there was no known treatment. Because of the easier accessibility, we had been attending Mass at a neighboring parish for several weeks. However, on that Sunday he insisted that we go to St. Anthony's, where we had gone for some thirty years. At the end of Mass, a woman whom I had never seen before nor have seen since, and whom I could not describe in any respect, handed me a printed card that I placed in my handbag. That evening I remembered the card and took it out to read. It was a "Prayer for Healing" from the Catholic Healing Ministry of Baltimore. On it was printed the name and phone number of Father Larry Gesy, who was the founder and moderator of the ministry.

I was suddenly aware of the "coincidence" of my learning of this ministry in such an unusual manner but such an appropriate time, and I felt urged to follow up on it. When I called Father Gesy at his rectory in Baltimore the next morning, I learned from his secretary that he was away for a few days with his mother, who was visiting from Iowa. She also had been diagnosed with cancer and was recovering from surgery.

I left my name and phone number with the secretary, and within a few hours he returned my call. I was very touched that in spite of his own personal suffering, Father Gesy had the time to return a call from a stranger. The kindness and compassion which I received as I related the situation of my husband's illness, I would discover, was a large part of the Healing Ministry.

The next Mass and healing service was to be held in Baltimore on the following Thursday, June 22, 1989. I made plans for us to attend that Mass, as my husband was still well enough to make the trip. Father Gesy mentioned, however, that should we not be able to attend, one of our children could go and pray by proxy. This is exactly what happened, as on that morning Al's condition began deteriorating.

Our son Chris and his wife, Lori, attended the service, and when they returned that night they were overwhelmed by its beauty. Just two days later, on June 24, the Lord called home our dearest husband, father, and grandfather. We had been married thirty-seven years with four children — Alfred, Jr., William, Christian, and Karen.

I had prayed, as had our whole family and so many of our friends, for his healing. He often mentioned how he felt surrounded by the love and prayers, and how he felt so comforted and peaceful. I had prayed so fervently and with enormous faith and hope that he would be physically healed. In my humanness I believed that my husband, a convert who had lived his faith to its fullest every day of his life, certainly "deserved" to be healed (although I know that none of us "deserve" anything except through the grace of God). He was young and vibrant and had so much to give in his profession as a dentist. I remember thinking, "All of my prayers, and he didn't live. Were my prayers not worthy enough to be answered?"

I had accepted that death is actually the ultimate healing we receive, and that my husband had reached the glory for which he was created. Still, I was deeply wounded by our loss.

In July I attended the Mass and healing service in Baltimore with some friends from Virginia. We met Father Gesy for the first time, and were received with great warmth. Each month that we attended our numbers grew as we spread the word. One night as we were returning home, I thought what a blessing it would be if Father Gesy could come to Virginia for a service. I decided to ask Monsignor Thomas Cassidy, the pastor of our church, for permission to invite Father Gesy. He very graciously consented, and in the fall the Catholic Healing Ministry of Baltimore came to St. Anthony's in Virginia for the first time and was welcomed by a large congregation.

The great response precipitated the next thought that we really should have more of the services and possibly such a ministry here in our diocese in Virginia. With much help from the late Reverend Arthur Verstraete, whom I had known for many years, and deacons Bob Curtin and Harry Brodeur, the groundwork was laid. Our plans and hopes were presented to our bishop and we were on our way to formation. The lay ministers were chosen from various parishes in the diocese, and the music ministry would be directed by Mark Forrest, then a student at Catholic University.

The final and most important task was to find a priest who would be our moderator. When Father Tuck Grinnell agreed, the Catholic Healing Ministry of Arlington, Virginia, was founded. We then realized that only the hand of the Lord could have directed all things to come together in such a precise way and in so short a time.

Our ministry, which is patterned after the one in Baltimore, has celebrated a Mass and healing service each month for the past five years throughout the many parishes of the diocese. There are twenty people on our team, which includes priests, deacons, and lay people. Priests are always available for the Sacrament of Reconciliation during the healing service. Many people who have been away from the sacraments for years take this occasion to seek their spiritual healing and return to the practice of their faith.

We often hear it said that God always answers our prayers, but sometimes not in the way that we expect. It is now clear to me that the healing that I had requested for my husband was ultimately given to me, and that God was really listening to my prayers. I received the grace not just to accept the cross that I would carry for the rest of my life, but to actually embrace it.

Through the formation of the Catholic Healing Ministry of Arlington, the healing power of Christ is passed on to the thousands of hurting people who have benefited spiritually, emotionally, and physically. In the tradition of our Faith, which recognizes that Christ is the Healer and we are but the instruments for Him, we are committed to bringing the healing love and compassion of our Lord to all who come to Him in faith and hope.

Father Larry Gesy

A journey of faith

ICCRS Healing Seminar and Evangelistic Outreach
San Giovanni Rotondo, Italy
October 3-7, 1995

uring the last week in January, 1994, I received a call from Catherine Griffin, the director of the Catholic Healing Ministry of Arlington (CHMA) located in Falls Church, Virginia. Catherine called to inform me that the International Catholic Charismatic Renewal Services (ICCRS), located in the Vatican, was sponsoring an international seminar on healing. Attendance was by invitation only! Had I been invited? No, I had not received an invitation. Catherine told me to watch the mail. At the time I was the interim pastor at St. Joseph Church in Taneytown, Maryland (until February, 1995).

Within a few days I received the invitation through the national Chariscenter office located in Locust Grove, Virginia, stating that I was one of the potential candidates for the ICCRS Healing Seminar. The theme of the seminar was to be: "Jesus called the twelve together, gave them power to overcome all demons and to cure disease. He sent them forth to proclaim the reign of God and to heal the afflicted."

I responded immediately to the invitation. I was excited, especially because San Giovanni Rotondo was the home of Padre Pio.

On February 14, 1995, I became the pastor of St. Francis of Assisi parish in Brunswick, Maryland, and St. Mary parish in Petersville, Maryland. God had given me another gift of these two beautiful country parishes in the tri-state area of Maryland, Virginia, and West Virginia, near the historic area of Harpers Ferry, West Virginia, and the Antietam battlefield, very close to Baltimore and Washington, D.C.

These two parishes are growing rapidly with many professional people building homes from where they can commute by train to their work in Washington, D.C. The commuter train is two blocks from the St. Francis rectory in Brunswick. Both parishes needed a great deal of healing and rejuvenating. I was pleased that Archbishop (now Cardinal) Keeler had entrusted me with this new mission as a pastor. This, too, was another journey of faith, and I felt that the seminar was very much a part of the new journey.

As I dug my heels into a parish that needed everything, I greatly anticipated the trip in October. In June, Father Ronald Pytel, my best priest friend, became seriously ill. Ron is the pastor of Holy Rosary Church in Baltimore and director of the archdiocesan shrine to Divine Mercy. He needed heart valve surgery. The surgery was scheduled immediately for June 14 at Johns Hopkins Hospital in Baltimore, Maryland. His heart specialist was Dr. Nicholas Fortuin and the surgeon Dr. Peter Green. Both doctors are the best in their fields. Trusting in Divine Mercy and Blessed Faustina, Father Ron had surgery. Recovery was slow, and his prognosis was uncertain because his heart had been seriously damaged before the surgery. Prior to my departure for Italy I was very worried. Yet I knew that God would give Father Ron the healing that he needed to continue his normal life and work as pastor of Holy Rosary. I took with me his petition for healing as well as a six-inch stack of petitions of parishioners and friends to place at the tomb of Padre Pio.

Monday, October 2, 1995

The time finally arrived. Catherine Griffin, the director of the CHMA, and I left for the seminar in Italy. Father Tuck Grinnell, the priest moderator of CHMA and the pastor of St. Anthony of Padua, was to meet us at the seminar.

The CHMA was founded five years ago based on the model of the Catholic Healing Ministry of Baltimore (CHMB). As the founder of both ministries, I was very happy to have representatives of both with me to share this first-time seminar on healing.

Tuesday, October 3, 1995

We arrived in Rome. It had been twenty years since I last was in the Eternal City. It was good to be back anticipating my twentieth anniversary of priesthood on October 11 and my twenty-first anniversary of ordination to the diaconate on October 12.

We arrived in San Giovanni after a very tiring six-hour trip by bus. We were in the beautiful mountainous countryside of southern Italy across the Adriatic Sea from Medjugorje. The town is isolated and very old, yet there is a spirit of peace, a spirit of Padre Pio. His presence permeates the entire community.

Six hundred people from seventy-four countries were present for the seminar. The Most Reverend Vincenzo d'Addoria, archbishop of the diocese in which San Giovanni Rotondo is located, welcomed us. He prayed that the Holy Spirit would pour out His gifts upon us and the seminar. The archbishop encouraged us to remain close to the Lord in the Eucharist and to Mary, His mother. Padre Pio's holiness was rooted in his love of the Eucharist and of Mary.

The seminar began with a "Welcome and Vision" by Charles Whitehead, President of ICCRS, and Sister Nancy Kellar, Director of ICCRS.

Charles Whitehead informed us that healing has always been connected with a shrine or a saint. God is raising up men and women today to bring healing to His people. He wants His people set free in body, soul, and spirit. Those present at the seminar, the clergy and laity from seventy-four countries, are being used as fragile and broken instruments to continue the mission of Jesus Christ. Hopefully our learning and our sharing from the seminar would enable us to enable others in the healing ministry.

Sister Nancy Kellar set the stage with the themes of the seminar:

1. Jesus *called* the twelve together. We are called to minister to one another. We need rest and time to be with each other on this seminar. Sister encouraged us to take advantage of the sacraments as well as private prayer, praise, and adoration in the chapel.

2. Jesus *empowered* the twelve to overcome all demons and to cure disease.

3. He *sent* them out to proclaim the reign of God and to heal the sick.

The icon of Our Lady of Perpetual Help was enshrined in the seminar room. Sister asked us to look upon it. It is about empowerment.

Wednesday, October 4, 1995, The Feast of St. Francis of Assisi
Sacraments and Healing

The speaker was Father Emilio Tardiff, M.S.C., author and worldwide preacher on healing. In James 5:13-15, the early

Church sent the elders to anoint the sick with oil and to pray for healing. This is the root of the sacrament of the Anointing of the Sick.

Ultimately the basis of all healing is the compassion of Jesus Christ, the Divine Healer, the Lord of Divine Mercy. Through the seven sacraments, as the expression of the Lord's compassion and healing, we are called to do as He did and to evangelize as He did so that all may believe. In the healings of Jesus, people see, believe, and are saved.

Since Vatican II, the Church does not look at the sacrament as the last unction but considers it also as a sacrament for the living. We know that only an ordained priest can administer the sacrament of the Anointing of the Sick, but this new perspective also calls for the laity to claim their vocation by praying for the sick, laying hands on the sick, and anointing them in the name of Jesus Christ.

The various gifts of the Spirit lead to healing. God is walking in our midst. How God heals in various ways! In the midst of miracles faith becomes contagious. Processions with the Blessed Sacrament, such as seen at Lourdes, are manifestations of Jesus walking in our midst as healer and liberator. Signs and miracles help us to believe in the presence of Jesus Christ in the world. The Real Presence is the *Real Presence*. But God's ways are not our ways. Sometimes He heals and sometimes He does not. It is in His will, as the instrument of healing, and not ours that we must trust.

Some of the greatest healings are in the presence of the *Real Presence*! Father Tardiff gave the following witness about healings that he had observed:

A little girl, who was told that her optic nerve was impaired, was healed in the midst of a Eucharistic healing service. Gradually her healing began and continued until she had total recovery. The doctor attested to an intervention and was informed that it was Jesus Christ who had healed her.

Another story was that of an elderly nun who had had to use

a hearing aid since an early age. She experienced a noise in her ear. As the same time, a second nun, her twin sister, with the same problem, came forward. Both received identical healing. The reporters and the doctors wanted an explanation. No natural explanation could be given. It was Jesus Christ who had healed them.

Father Tardiff related an account of the healing power of the Sacrament of Reconciliation: A man brought his wife to Father Tardiff. For months she had been unable to eat or sleep. He heard her confession and absolved her. Afterwards she came to the rectory where she ate and drank like one who was starved. Her husband saw and believed. The power of the sacrament had brought inner healing. Many psychosomatic diseases are cured in the Sacrament of Penance.

An account was given of the evangelizing of seven Muslims who were present at a healing service. They saw, believed, and converted to Catholicism immediately. Pre-evangelization would have taken months. This was instantaneous.

Once Father Tardiff kissed a child while giving the Holy Eucharist to the child's mother. The child, who had been deaf from birth, was healed. God had given Father Tardiff a "Word of Knowledge" to stop and kiss the child.

One time a woman was healed when she was hit by a falling papal flag.

In the panel discussion which followed the question was raised: Why are there so few healings in parishes? The consensus was that most people are afraid of healing, including the priests who have been sacramentally anointed as healers. In spite of our doubts, fears, and lack of understanding, God is calling teams of people to pray in expectation of healings.

These teams, when joined with the priests, can bring the community of believers to the bedsides of the sick. The charisms of the Holy Spirit are upon a community of believers in which all the individual gifts are joined for the common good of the sick.

Often we pray for healing and then are afraid that it will not happen. We need faith. Be obedient to what God gives us and be His humble servants. He will heal in His way and in His time. Fear is the opposite of love.

There is a danger today for clergy, laity, and doctors to compartmentalize faith and medicine. We should not put God in a box. Holistic healing involves faith and medicine healing the whole person.

Holiness in the life of the minister of healing

Another speaker was Dr. Philippe Madre, husband, father, doctor, and member of the Catholic community of the Beatitudes in France.

Dr. Madre stated that the life of the minister is very delicate. The charisms of healing vary from person to person, from one group to another, but the charisms are needed in a broken world. There is a new strength from the Holy Spirit coming to the Church and to the world. Be open to God moving in our lives.

The charism of healing is a free gift of the Holy Spirit. In itself the gift is not a grace of sanctification. It is in the exercising of the charism that one becomes holy.

God gives us prophecy, word of knowledge, discernment, charism, and fruits of the Spirit for sanctification. As long as we desire to love and use the gifts of the Spirit the more our ministry, the charisms, and our holiness shall grow.

Dr. Madre gave six signs of the integration of our ministry with the ministry of Jesus Christ:

1. The need to live a personal life in contemplative and inner peace. The inner life is the nourishment of our ministry. The healing ministry involves more than praying with the sick, it requires that we take more time with God to be renewed, strengthened, and rejuvenated. God teaches in solitude. God wants to speak to our hearts and to our souls more and more each day. To the heart comes guidance and teaching and from the heart go the gifts of the Spirit. The inside must equal the outside. Fruits

are produced from solitude — ministries grow. The opposite is also true — ministries die because of lack of solitude and peace.

2. There must be a community — a team — who joins in prayer and support for the minister. The power and the fruits of the Holy Spirit operate more fully and freely in a community.

3. We need to renew our life in the sacraments and so to evangelize the world. On October 3, the Holy Father spoke to us from his encyclical of the need for a new evangelization, in which we proclaim Christ, serve in charity, and celebrate the love of Jesus Christ by our lives, our prayer, and praise. New charisms will flow from the celebration of Jesus Christ.

4. The minister, the one who exercises the ministry, needs a spiritual confessor. The minister will have to fight many battles and temptations. The devil will do anything he can to stop the impact of God's servants in the ministry.

5. There are temptations in the ministry: a) Pride: We believe that God operates through us only. b) Tiredness and discouragement: Nothing goes as expected. When our prayers are not answered we can be tempted to unbelief. The devil wants us to become discouraged that we are stupid and wasting our time. c) Stubbornness: We believe that we have the same power as a doctor, that if we pray for someone, that person should and must be healed. We tell God what to do and how to do it. d) Emotional attachment: The minister can develop an attachment to the sick person, and the healer then is too affective and becomes ineffective.

6. Our ministry must pass from intercession to confession on our lips, growing spiritually in our hearts.

There is no set way of praying for the sick person. The Holy Spirit asks us to move with feeling for the sick, with an emotion of his heart. Being able to empathize with the sick person is the key to being a great instrument of healing. The compassion of Christ for the sick and the suffering moved the sick to trust and seek His healing touch. In their trust, they were healed. Jesus asks us to be one in unity with the suffering. This is the core of the Eucharistic body of Christ. It was the compassion and mercy of Jesus Christ that brought others to believe in the love of the Father.

There was a great diversity of charism in the five bishops, one hundred and sixty-two priests, numerous deacons, and all the laity present. I am reminded of Eucharistic Prayer III: that we are gathered from "east to west" in the common bond of Jesus Christ.

As it was the feast of St. Francis of Assisi, I remembered especially the people of St. Francis of Assisi parish in Brunswick, Maryland. I couldn't fail to mention, too, all the special friends of St. Francis, the animals. I thanked God for Domino and Dimi, my cherished Dalmatian friends. (Look at the back of this book for the picture of both of them.)

I remembered in a special way all the Sisters of St. Francis from Clinton, Iowa, who taught me at Our Lady of Good Counsel in Fonda, Iowa. I was in the third grade when I realized I had a vocation. It was their encouragement that had a impact on my life. May the life of this saint transform our lives that we may be instruments of his peace.

Thursday, October 5, 1995
Charisms and healing

The speaker was Dr. Jean Pliya, from Djougou, Benin, Africa.

Dr. Pliya began with the Scripture passage from Romans 5. He said that all healing comes from God. It is a free gift given to all Christians. The Christian can pray for his own healing, including liberation from occult bondage, oppression, obsession, and the demonic. Healings lead to evangelization of the world in the name of Jesus Christ. People see and believe and are saved. When people with charisms of healing pray over people, they are converted.

Healing has nothing to do with the holiness of the person

with the gift. God uses us in spite of our weaknesses. Thousands have been brought to the Lord in one service of prayer and praise. We read in Mark 16:15-18 that Jesus told His disciples to "Go into the whole world and proclaim the gospel to every creature. Whoever believes and is baptized will be saved; whoever does not will be condemned. These signs will accompany those who believe: in my name they will cast out demons; they will speak new languages. They will pick up serpents [with their hands] and if they drink any deadly thing, it will not harm them. They will lay their hands on the sick, and they will recover." The Good News of Jesus Christ penetrates even the most hardened of hearts. Conversion and penance are the fruits of healing.

Often people are not healed because of idols — paganism, spiritism, occultism, New Age, Satanism, etc. The idols in our lives must go before true conversion can take place. Penance and reconciliation must follow in our lives.

The Good News must be exhorted, confirmed, taught, and proclaimed with the charism of wisdom. The charism of the word of wisdom gives us the ability to understand the Word of the Lord. Once a priest came to Dr. Pliya with a personal problem. He opened the Bible and came across the passage about the wisdom of little children. The priest was too arrogant and proud. He agreed that he needed more humility in his life. He thanked Dr. Pliya and left much happier.

The second charism of Mark is speaking in tongues. The third charism is the discernment of evil spirits. Praying in tongues gives power over evil spirits. The last charism from Mark is the laying on of hands. It can be used by all people for healing. Touch is powerful and certainly so when used by two or more gathered in prayer.

The blessed sacramental oil is a special sign of healing. Anyone can use it. This is not to be confused with the oil of the infirm, which can be used only by a priest in the sacrament of the Anointing of the Sick. One day Dr. Pliya had a sick woman come to him at a charismatic meeting in France. She was still in deep grief and mourning over the death of her husband nine years previous. She was unable to travel or do much of anything. She was healed with the blessed oil. A woman with bleeding also was healed at this gathering by using the blessed oil.

Authentic charisms of the group and the "word of knowledge" can be a Scripture passage, a color, warmth, cold, an image that gives us insight and discernment. Sometimes the healer experiences the pain of the person being healed. After the healing, the pain disappears in the healer. He can also recognize and discern evil spirits in a person.

If a healing is authentic, it is necessary to discern the source of the healing. Is it from Jesus Christ, self, or the devil? Satan can mimic the gifts of God. By their fruits the healings shall be known.

Resting in the Spirit is a deep healing of God. A person may lose control of muscles, speaking, moving, etc., and lie on the floor. This resting can bring deep inner healing with many fruits. These miracles are the manifestations of the gifts given to the apostles themselves.

Dr. Pliya related this story: One day a Muslim woman came to a healing service. She was on crutches and wanted to see Jesus. "Where is Jesus?" she screamed. "Is this him?" as she pointed to the priest. She was told that if she went to the church she would see Jesus. Being a Muslim, she could not receive the Anointing of the Sick. Still, she was prayed over. Her legs began to shake. The group stood her up. God's honor was at stake. She was being held up. Dr. Pliya went to the Eucharist and asked God what to do. He discerned that God told him to tell her to walk. She left the church without crutches that evening. This news of her healing was badly received by her Muslim friends. She now is baptized, a Catholic, and a disciple of Jesus Christ. Praise the Lord.

The healing ministry begins when we have the compassion of Jesus Christ. Compassion is not sympathy but the true love of Jesus Christ for the person in need. Examples of this include Jesus healing the blind man with the paste made with spittle, or a sick person touching the hem of the garment of the Lord or one of His apostles.

Sacramentals are very powerful in healing. Medals, holy water, blessed oil, crucifixes, relics, the monstrance, the Bible, etc., have been used for centuries to bring healing and deliverance from the devil and temptation. Healings can be instantaneous, days later, weeks, or months later.

Healing does not depend on the doubt or the faith of the sick person. What is important is the prayer and our faith for the sick person. We must reach out in faith with trust. We must never make a healing service a show centered around the healings. Our service must be centered on prayer with our eyes on Jesus the Divine Healer as the source of our power. We must not control methods or styles or the prayer of a team member. Do not imitate anyone else. Let the Holy Spirit lead you to a style of healing that is unique and individual to each person. Do not build false hopes in people. Be cautious not to feel that you are the healer doing it on your own. It must be in the climate of exultation not exaltation. Do not expect people to give witness to their healings. It can be a violation of their privacy. Remember it was not the healings of Jesus Christ that saved the world but His suffering on the cross!

Our prayer life must be with Jesus Christ, the Eucharist, Mary, and the saints. We must live in humility without the approval of others or comparing our charism with others. We want people to follow Jesus, not run after us. The healing ministry demands that we also must bear the suffering and the cross of Jesus Christ. Daily prayer is necessary. God's gifts don't depend on our gifts or our efforts, in spite of it all. As the mystical body we must be prudent yet *bold* with the gifts. Let us live in obedience of the Church and in the love of the Lord. After all, it is love that does not come to an end.

Dr. Pliya spoke about the "word of knowledge" as a gift of

the Holy Spirit. Reading hearts is not an accurate understanding. The priest or minister of healing receives the word of knowledge in his heart, which he then relates to the person. An example would be Padre Pio, who could relate to the problems of a penitent. The Curé of Ars had the same gift. They had the ability by the word of wisdom to touch the hearts of people, to see into their souls and to call the penitent to conversion.

It is the charism of the word of knowledge that demands we die to self. We do not have any certitude about the source of the discernment. It can come from God or from the devil. St. Paul says that we must verify healings. Some are easy to verify and others are not. The medical sciences must be used for verification. If we are not certain of a healing, we must get medical verification before witness may be given. The word of knowledge, when confirmed by testimony, really builds up the people's faith and brings them to Jesus Christ. If the healing can be verified immediately, then we ask for testimony. An example of this was in Venezuela. Dr. Pliya had the word of knowledge about the blindness of a man in his left eye. The man came forward, was healed, and then read Scripture with the left eye.

The word of knowledge is becoming more prominent in the world today. In Peru, fourteen thousand people attended an evangelization and healing service. After the Mass, Dr. Pliya prayed for the sick. He received a word of knowledge that a paralyzed person was in need of healing. Nothing happened. He continued to pray. Nothing happened. The word of knowledge came that the paralyzed man was deaf and in a wheelchair. God healed him of his deafness and then he walked. Medically he had been stricken with paralysis and deafness at the same time. He asked God to heal the man of his deafness first so that he could hear the command to walk. Praise the Lord for His gifts. Many a prophet and many a saint would have loved to see what we have seen in our time.

Doctrinal discernment is important. In doctrinal discernment we use personal and communal judgment to evaluate the fruits of the spirit. By the fruit a tree will be known. Scripture, the teachings of the church, doctrine, and dogma as well as the magisterium must be used for doctrinal discernment. Charismatic discernment evaluates the free gifts of the Spirit.

An example of this would be a man in the Dominican Republic who had a healing thirteen years ago. One and a half years later he could no longer walk as before. The man came to see Dr. Pliya at a retreat in his parish. They prayed. Dr. Pliya received the word of knowledge — a charismatic discernment — that this was not a disease. They prayed for deliverance of demonic oppression, then bound the spirit and sent it to Jesus Christ and claimed the healing. The man got up and walked as normal. He was not sick but was being attacked by a spirit that wanted to stop the man from giving witness to his healing.

Later that afternoon we went to the tomb of Padre Pio to celebrate Mass at the church of Our Lady of Grace. We walked up the hill to the church, a real climb. I carried all the petitions to the tomb of Padre Pio. On the hill is the church and the medical hospital. It is a very impressive sight. Millions of pilgrims come yearly to the church and the hospital for healing. I found my way to the lower church and the tomb of Padre Pio. The coffin is a large, smoky-black marble surrounded by a tall black iron barrier.

Many pilgrims were at the tomb praying, some leaving flowers. The mood was very serene and reverent. I left the enormous stack of petitions by pushing them through the iron-enclosed fence. These petitions were from parishioners from St. Francis of Assisi in Brunswick and St. Mary in Petersville, my two parishes. Many were from friends. I said a very special prayer for Father Ron Pytel to receive a complete healing.

The following is excerpted from the conference booklet on the "Life of Padre Pio" by Father Augustin McGregor, OCSO:

When we say that Padre Pio was a charismatic figure we immediately place him in a certain category of persons who in some way are outstanding by reason of supernatural powers and gifts which they possess through the Holy Spirit. This is not to say that the gifts of "charismata," as they are called, are primarily extraordinary or, in any exclusive sense, limited to a special group of persons in the Church. Indeed the gifts of God are of infinite variety and their distribution in the Church is unlimited according as the Spirit "blows wherever he pleases" (Jn 3:8). But at the same time, the Church has always held that besides the gifts and graces received by the faithful for the living of the Christian life there are others of a manifestly more supernatural nature bestowed by God on certain specially chosen individuals.

In the life of a charismatic like Padre Pio undoubtedly there were "signs and wonders" (Acts 2:43), such as the sacred stigmata or the inspiring dawn celebration of the Eucharistic Sacrifice. Many people — lost in modern man's complex search for light and meaning — came out of curiosity, little realizing that the mercy of a loving God operates even through curiosity. They came to witness these signs and wonders for themselves. In his wounds they saw once more the "blood of Jesus" which since the days of Calvary has been purifying us from all sin (1Jn 1:7). In his Mass they saw man and God in unspeakable communication. How often during this Mass did it seem as if some vehement argument were being thrashed out as he bargained and pleaded with God for the souls of men and women! Surprised, astonished, tear-stained, crushed beneath the unbearable sorrow of repentance, they saw in this victim soul a glimpse of the Eternal Shepherd going after His lost sheep. In this voice they heard an echo of the Lord reaching down the ages, calling out to men and women . . . inviting them: "Come to me. . . ."

Padre Pio was a prophet of the times. He discerned the massive shift away from God as well as the deliberate effort by many so-called Christians to drop the whole idea of the Cross. As a prophet he spoke out boldly against these false trends. Not, of course, in so many words, but rather by his "lived" proclamation of the Word. In season and out, he was telling us how Jesus not only loved us but did so by the supreme sacrifice of suffering and dying for us. His life told us that His agony and sacrifice did not cease at the historical moment of Calvary but reaches far beyond it to embrace all the centuries and all the ages of mankind.

We can so easily forget what was accomplished so long ago on the Cross and it seems that in the providence of God there should always be men and women of the same caliber as Padre Pio to be forceful reminders of Calvary.

Documented accounts of cures and miracles of healings both bodily and spiritually clearly attest to the presence of other unusual gifts in Padre Pio. All were given by God and exercised by His servant on behalf of all who had come to know the surpassing love to be found in Christ Jesus.

But besides these extraordinary gifts of Padre Pio let us not forget the many others, less discernible perhaps to the unobservant eye, no less remarkable for all that. For instance, the sublime gift to bear heavy suffering day in and day out for prolonged periods; or the willingness to spend oneself for long hours cramped in the physically restricted area of a tiny confessional. His utterances of wisdom and knowledge (cf. 1 Cor 12:8), his sayings, his words of exhortation and consolation (Rm 12:8) were an inspiration for so many. All of these, too, must be viewed from a charismatic perspective for they are in the order of gifts received from the Holy Spirit.

There is, however, one charism which has not received the attention it merits and that is the gift of "spiritual father."

Padre Pio was indeed truly a father, exercising rights, duties, and responsibilities similar to those of fathers in the temporal order.

Once he said to one of his spiritual children: "You think you know my love for you. But you don't know that it is much greater than you can imagine. I follow you with my prayer, with my suffering and with my tears."

For when all is said and done, beyond all the rare charismata and extraordinary spiritual phenomena, it was love that was the essence of Padre Pio's life and activity, the very foundation of all he taught. Let the love which he demonstrated in his life and taught to his children be the monument by which he will always be remembered. He would desire nothing else. On the fiftieth anniversary of his first

Mass he said: "I desire nothing other than to love, to suffer another fifty years for my brothers and sisters, to burn for all with Thee, Lord, with Thee on the Cross." We may certainly implore Padre Pio in Heaven to teach us this love for it is the "bond which makes us perfect" (Col 3:4).

— *Augustin McGregor*

Later in the afternoon, the pews from the church were moved into the church square for Mass with Bishop Cordes from Germany. Thousands of people gathered to celebrate Mass. Bishop Cordes reminded the congregation gathered to evangelize the world by example, prayer, and proclamation that all might hear the Word of God. We must not be afraid but must be bold. This is the way Padre Pio lived.

Later I went to the old church and the living area of Padre Pio. The present new church is attached to the old church and the monastery. I visited the cell of Padre Pio. It was very austere in the spirit of poverty of St. Francis of Assisi.

Deliverance ministry

The evening talk featured speakers Father Tardiff and Dr. Pliya:

In Luke 11 we are given authority over demonic spirits and the devil. One of the proofs that the kingdom of God is in our midst is the casting out of demons. The apostles were empowered to cast out demons. It is not the devil's kingdom because he is destroyed by Jesus Christ on the cross. It is important to be balanced on the existence and the presence of the devil. We should not deny his existence nor should we exaggerate his power. Pope Paul VI in 1972 clearly stated the reality of the devil.

Demonic possession is very rare, but it does exist. A woman in France was dedicated in a demonic sect to the devil. She was sent to the church by the sect to steal the Eucharist for black masses. She had even signed a covenant in her blood to Satan. Father Tardiff exorcised her by the permission of the bishop of the diocese. She went to confession and was delivered. It is common for children to be dedicated to Satan so that they may have power as witches or Satanists. Some children are dedicated in the womb.

Father Tardiff said that every diocese should have an official exorcist. Many bishops will not deal with the issue. This is an injustice to the people in bondage. Keep in mind, he said, that only a priest delegated by his bishop can perform an official exorcism. It is the authority of the bishop that is the power over Satan.

Demonic possession is surrendering one's free will to the devil. Our free will is God's greatest gift as His baptised children. Oppression and obsession are the influence of the devil on our thoughts, our minds, and our bodies. An example of this is persistent temptation. Another example is of a boy who wanted to commit suicide. He was prayed over for deliverance and was freed of the desire.

Any baptized person can pray for himself or others for deliverance from the power of evil. Be cautious, Father Tardiff said. Because it is sometimes difficult to determine the difference between a psychological disease and an obsession or oppression, prayerful discernment is crucial. Great harm can be done to a person by blaming a medical problem on the devil. We must be balanced in examining all aspects of a person's need.

For deliverance, a good confession of our faults is important. Forgiveness and love is necessary. Clean out the house and burn all occult objects and materials. Close the door to the demonic by prayer and a strong free will. Healing takes a long time, like the preparation of the soil for the seed. Put out a sign on your door, "No Rooms for Rent. This House Is Occupied by Jesus Christ." Ask for the protection of Jesus Christ with boldness.

(For a more complete coverage of this topic, read chapter nine, "Infestation, Obsession, Possession" found in my first book *Today's Destructive Cults and Movements*, published in 1993 by Our Sunday Visitor.)

Friday, October 6, 1995
Emotional healing and psychology

The speaker was Dr. Michele Greischar, wife, mother, psychotherapist, and lecturer from the United States.

Dr. Greischar started her talk by telling us about being in graduate school in Chicago. One day a priest asked everyone to read the Scripture passage on Pentecost. Inside her a fire began when she read the passage. This passage transformed her life. She realized that God wanted her to follow Him in the charismatic renewal.

She developed her private practice in psychology. She prayed daily for her clients. Her training was contrary to her faith about praying for clients. Yet, she continued and asked her clients if they wanted prayer. Clients with prayer healed quickly and therapy was hastened.

Most inner healing is the fact that God loved us first. Paul says: "Put on the new self." Christian therapy is about shedding the old self, dying to the old, and rising to the new life of the cross. In professional therapy there can be a contradiction between embracing the cross and self help. Therapy wants us to go back to the roots of childhood and into the later years. Christian therapy asks us to embrace the cross and allow Christ to walk with us through the hurt and the pain. Professional therapy is centered on method and various philosophies, whereas Christian therapy is centered on compassion and the loving hand of Jesus Christ. He can heal in a brief moment with prayer what would take weeks, months, and even years in therapy.

Listening prayer is critical. It is easy with the burdens of ministry to become overloaded. Yet we are called to listen with the compassion and patience of Jesus Christ. An example of this was a twenty-five-year-old woman who had been running from relationships, abusing drugs and alcohol. She herself was unwanted, the result of an "unsuccessful" abortion. Her whole life reflected this image. Now, at this stage in her life, she is embracing the pain rather than running away. She is putting on the "new self."

As little children, we were inhibited from and discouraged from exploring. We should encourage all people to explore their lives regardless of age. It is in tracing the family roots that we see the source of the behavior. Healing comes to a whole family when the members are able to look into their lives and trust Jesus. The family situation is very effective way to balance therapy and prayer.

Another example is of a man, a lawyer, who had been having panic attacks. The attacks seemed to be due to stress at work with the partners. Occult practices were a part of his past. He sought counseling and prayer. The prayer team was called in. The next day his sister called and told him she had decided to do something about her addiction to prescription drugs. This is a family-based method that enables the entire family to be healed with prayer and therapy.

As ministers of healing it is important to ask, "What would Jesus do in the life of the person in this situation?" If we can unite with the will and the hurt of the person, embrace the family, we will be able to empower the family and ourselves to be emotionally and spiritually healthy. Do we feel like Jesus and Mary in our ministry? If so, we can unite their cross with ours, walk with Jesus and Mary in their suffering of pain on this earth. There can be no pride, deception, or hidden agendas in our lives if we are to be instruments of healing. We must be like Lazarus in John 11. We die to the old self and come out of the tomb with a new life.

After the conference, Catherine Griffin, Father Lou from Canada, and I traveled to the Basilica of St. Michael the Archangel in the Gargano region about an hour south of San Giovanni Rotondo. Our cab driver pointed out to us along the way the original church. It was here that the town got its name. The church was in the round, a rotunda. It was the belief that St. John embraced the entire world when he was entrusted to Mary and Mary to him when Jesus was on the cross. He is the disciple who represents all of mankind. The cab driver informs us that many of the saints including St. Francis of Assisi walked for weeks, sometimes months, on pilgrimage to this shrine.

The shrine to St. Michael the Archangel is the oldest in the world. St. Michael appeared in 490 to Elvio Emanuele, Lord of Monte Gargano. St. Michael appeared at this shrine again in 492, 493, and 1656. The area was the site of a pagan cult. St. Michael asked that a shrine be built in his name. The grotto was never consecrated according to the laws of the Church because it had already been done by the Angelic Minister on his third apparition in 493. During the centuries the pontiffs have declared it a Basilica, Celestial Basilica, and Archcathedral.

A large, church-like entrance leads down carved stone steps to the actual shrine, which is a cave. As the stone steps lead deeper into the earth, the walls along the steps become very interesting. Painted frescos adorned the walls until pilgrims took particles of paintings believing in the curative power of the saints that the fresco portrayed. There were carvings on the entire walls, some going back to the age of the crusades. All crusaders came to the shrine invoking the protection and power of St. Michael.

St. Francis journeyed to Monte St. Angelo, as the town was called in 1216, begging the Angelic Pardon of St. Michael. It is said that the saint felt too unworthy to enter the grotto and instead kissed the entrance and engraved a Tau cross on an altar. This can be seen to this day.

The promise of St. Michael is that every prayer will be granted at the shrine. I prayed for all my parishioners, those who had sent petitions with me, friends, and especially Father

Ron for a complete healing. This shrine is very touching to me especially because of the power of St. Michael the Archangel in my the ministry dealing with the occult.

Saturday, October 7, 1995

The members of the conference traveled by bus to a stadium in Foggia, about an hour away. The stadium was to be the gathering sight for a healing service for twenty-three thousand people or more. And me? I went to Lanciano, Italy, with Catherine and Fathers Gerry and Brandon from New Jersey. Lanciano is the home of the Eucharistic Miracle of the Real Presence. I have preached this miracle for years as the scientific proof of the Real Presence body and blood, soul and divinity, God and man.

For more than twelve centuries the first, and the most important, of the miracles of the Eucharist in the Catholic Church has been preserved in the town of Lanciano. The prodigious event took place in the eighth century in the little church of San Legonziano.

In about the year 700, a Basilian monk in Lanciano, Italy, had a continuous doubt about the Real Presence of Christ in the Eucharist. He could not bring himself to believe that at the words of consecration uttered by him as a priest over the bread and the wine

Photo courtesy of Father Larry Gesy

The Sanctuary of the Eucharistic Miracle at Lanciano, Italy.

their substance became the Body and Blood of Christ. But being a devout priest he continued to celebrate the liturgy of the Mass according to the teaching of the Church. He begged God to remove his doubt.

One day, as he celebrated Mass, following the words of the consecration, the bread literally changed into Flesh and the wine into Blood. At first he was overwhelmed by what he saw. Then, regaining his composure, he called the faithful present to come to the altar to see what the Lord had caused to happen.

The changed substances were not consumed. The bread-turned-Flesh, and the wine-turned-Blood, which later coagulated into five irregular globules, were first placed in a precious ivory container. In 1713, they were enshrined in an artistic silver monstrance of the Naples School in which they are preserved even to the present day at the Church of St. Francis in Lanciano.

Many years later, the Church, wanting to ascertain the true nature of the substances, requested scientists to examine them and give a verdict. In November, 1970, a team of medical experts was convened to begin the investigation. It was chaired by Professor Odoardo. At the start of the investigation he was very skeptical of the matter, but by the middle of December he sent his first message to the Director of the Shrine. It was a very brief but dramatic telegram: IN THE BEGINNING WAS THE WORD. AND THE WORD WAS MADE FLESH.

On March 4, 1971, the complete report was ready. The analyses verified the following:

The Flesh is real flesh. The Blood is real blood.

The Flesh consists of the muscular tissue of the heart (myocardium).

The Flesh and Blood belong to the human species.

The Flesh and Blood have the same blood type (AB).

In the Blood there were found proteins in the same normal proportions (percentage-wise) as are found in the makeup of fresh normal blood.

In the Blood there were found also these minerals: chlorides, phosphorus, magnesium, potassium, sodium, and calcium.

The preservation of the Flesh and Blood, which were left in their natural state for twelve centuries (i.e. without any chemical preservatives) and exposed to the action of atmospheric and biological agents, remains an extraordinary phenomenon.

It may be said in conclusion that science, when called to testify, has given a positive response to the authenticity of the Eucharistic Miracle of Lanciano.

The sanctuary is now run by the Frati Conventuali Minor di San Francesco (Franciscan Conventual Friars). It was moving, after climbing a flight of stairs, to view the monstrance, enclosed behind glass. We then celebrated Mass at the altar where the miracle had happened. I offered Mass for all parishioners and friends. This was a truly an encounter in faith with the *Real Presence.*

On November 3, 1974, Pope John Paul II, then Cardinal of Krakow, after venerating the Holy Relics expressed his devotion in the shrine guest register thus: "Make us always to believe more in you, and to love you" (Eucharistic Hymn of St. Thomas).

(This information is taken from a reprint from the *Marian Helpers Bulletin*, Volume

Photo courtesy of Father Larry Gesy

The Monstrance which holds the Eucharistic Miracle.

XXXIX, No. 1, Association of Marian Helpers, Congregation of Marians, Stockbridge, Massachusetts 01263.)

The next day the Pope was in Baltimore and I was in Italy! When we returned to San Giovanni, I was asked by Father Gerry to be the celebrant of the Saturday vigil Mass at the tomb of Padre Pio. I couldn't believe it. The Gospel for that Sunday was about having faith strong enough to move the sycamore tree. The entire mountainside there is covered with sycamore trees. Many have been uprooted in this town.

Those who went to the stadium in Foggia were overwhelmed with the outpouring of the Holy Spirit on nearly thirty thousand people. Many were healed and thousands had the Gospel preached to them. This was a perfect example of the healing and evangelization that the Holy Father was talking about.

Sunday, October 8, 1995

The conference was over, and we were departing for the four corners of the world. The conference had been excellent. We learned that the Holy Spirit is truly working and giving witness by the varied ministries of people from the U.S., the Congo, Hungary, Korea, the Philippines, and all inclusive of the seventy-four countries present.

Father Tuck, Catherine, and I went to Florence by train, the city of the Renaissance, Dante, Galileo, and Michelangelo, who are buried in the church of San Croce. This has to be one of the most classically beautiful cities in the world. I love Florence for its art, especially the Uffizi Gallery — the works of Michelangelo and the Cathedral of Santa Maria de Fiore just to name a few. The cathedral is the fruit of the commitment of a large number of such artists as Cambio, Giotto, Pisano, and Brunelleschi, who worked on the church for centuries beginning in 1296. At night, lighted, it is magnificent. It looks like the gates of heaven, especially when viewed while eating Italian ice cream.

Wednesday, October 11, 1995

We said good-bye to Florence, on overload from the endless art and shops with their beautiful exhibits and the fine art in the open-air markets. October 12 was the twenty-first anniversary of my ordination to the diaconate. This day, October 11, was the twentieth anniversary of my ordination to priesthood.

We toured Rome at night with a priest friend of Father Tuck. It had been twenty years since I was last here, before my ordination to the priesthood. The impression of the Eternal City has always lingered on my mind. We viewed the city at night from one of the hilltops near the Vatican. Rome has such a history. It is almost possible to envision the city before Christ, the underground Church during the early persecutions, the founding of the Church on the rock of Peter. It was upon the tomb of Peter that the first church of Christendom was built, now St. Peter's at the Vatican. The next day we would be celebrating Mass at the tomb of St. Peter, where Christianity began its spread through Europe.

As we passed the Vatican that evening, the lights were on in the Pope's study. He had returned safely from the United States.

Thursday, October 12, 1995

Catherine and I met Father Gerry and Father Brandon in St. Peter's Square. When they arrived we went into St. Peter's. We found the sacristy to vest for Mass and then were taken by altar boys down the steps under the main altar of St. Peter to a very small but beautiful chapel. In front of me was the tomb of St. Peter. It had always been my dream to celebrate Mass on the tomb of St. Peter. It is almost impossible to be allowed to do this, but thanks to my friends, this happened. I believe that all the extraordinary events of this trip would not have happened even if I had planned them. I felt so blessed and so grateful for these special graces, especially on my anniversaries.

In the late 1960s, archeological digging confirmed that Peter, after his martyrdom, was actually buried on the site traditionally claimed as his tomb. In A.D. 313, Constantine ended the persecution of the Church. He built the basilica on the tomb of Peter, the rock of the Church.

The Mass began and I was handed the Lectionary to proclaim the Gospel: "You are Peter, and upon this rock I will build my church, and the gates of the netherworld shall not prevail against it." Never before had those words from the Gospel of Matthew 16:18 had such an impact. After Mass, we toured the Vatican Gardens, saw the Vatican Museum, and concluded with the newly restored Sistine Chapel. It is just as beautiful, bright, and colorful as in the days when Michelangelo painted it.

After viewing the Sistine, Catherine and I went to the Basilica of Santa Maria de Angelo. This is the titular church of His Eminence William H. Keeler, the Archbishop of the Archdiocese of Baltimore. Cardinal Keeler was elevated to a cardinal in April by Pope John Paul II. The basilica is very impressive, with a long history. Prior to Christianity it was a public bath and the site of many a martyr's death. Later, when Christianized, the bath became a church. This basilica was one of the last works of Michelangelo.

This had been an unbelievable day, an unbelievable conference, an unbelievable trip, a true journey of faith. I was reminded of Father Tardiff's comment that many prophets and saints would have longed to see in their time what we are seeing today through the eyes of faith. Many miracles happen every day when we serve the Lord. He showers His graces upon us as if every day is Christmas.

Friday, October 13, 1995

We left Rome. In conclusion, I would like to end this journey of faith with a passage from *The Liturgy of the Hours*, Volume IV, page 206: "From the beginning of a sermon on the beatitudes by Saint Leo the Great, pope" (Sermo 95, 1-2: PL 54, 461-462):

Dearly beloved, when our Lord Jesus Christ was preaching the Gospel of the kingdom and healing various illnesses throughout the whole of Galilee, the fame of his mighty works spread into all of Syria, and great crowds from all parts of Judea flocked to the heavenly physician. Because human ignorance is slow to believe what it does not see, and equally slow to hope for what it does not know, those who were to be instructed in the divine teaching had first to be aroused by bodily benefits and visible miracles so that, they would no longer doubt the wholesome effect of his doctrine. In order, therefore, to transform outward healings into inward remedies, and to cure men's souls now that He had healed their bodies, our Lord separated himself from the surrounding crowds, climbed to the solitude of a neighboring mountain, and called the apostles to himself. From the height of this mystical site He then instructed them in the most lofty doctrines, suggesting both by the very nature of the place and by what He was doing that it was He who long ago had honored Moses by speaking to Him. Then His words evidenced a terrifying justice, but now they reveal a sacred compassion, in order to fulfill what was promised in the words of the prophet Jeremiah: *Behold the days are coming, says the Lord, when I shall establish a new covenant with the house of Israel and with the house of Judah. After those days, says the Lord, I shall put my laws within them and write them on their hearts.*

And so it was that He who had spoken to Moses spoke also to the apostles. Writing in the hearts of His disciples, the swift hand of the Word composed the ordinances of the new covenant. And this was not done as formerly, in the midst of dense clouds, amid terrifying sounds and lightning, so that the people were frightened away from approaching the mountain. Instead, there was a tranquil discourse which clearly reached the ears of all who stood nearby so that the harshness of the law might be softened by the gentleness of grace, and the spirit of adoption might dispel the terror of slavery.

Concerning the content of Christ's teaching, His own sacred words bear witness; thus whoever longs to attain eternal blessedness can now recognize the steps that lead to that high happiness. Blessed, he says, are the poor in spirit, for theirs is the kingdom of heaven. It might have been unclear to which poor he was referring, if after the words blessed are the poor, he had not added anything about the kind of poor he had in mind. For then the poverty that many suffer because of grave and harsh necessity might seem sufficient to merit the kingdom of heaven. But when he says: Blessed are the poor in spirit, he shows that the kingdom of heaven is to be given to those who are distinguished by their humility of soul rather than by their lack of worldly goods.

Are the prayers of the humble of heart answered? You will have to read Father Ron's chapter regarding his extraordinary answer to prayers — the total healing of his heart!

My special thanks to Father Gerry Ruane, Father Brendan Williams and Kasmiera (Cass) Hryckiewicz, who introduced me to these two fine priests and who gave me the pictures that are included with this chapter. I am indebted to them for their kindness. In addition I thank all the staff of ICCRS for creating the tremendous experience of faith which was this Conference. The enclosures from the Conference are used here thanks to ICCRS.

Prayers

The Sign of the Cross
In the name of the Father, and of the Son, and of the Holy Spirit. Amen.

Our Father
Our Father, who art in heaven, hallowed be thy name. Thy kingdom come; thy will be done on earth as it is in heaven.
Give us this day our daily bread; and forgive us our trespasses as we forgive those who trespass against us; and lead us not into temptation, but deliver us from evil. Amen.

Hail Mary
Hail, Mary, full of grace, the Lord is with thee; blessed art thou among women, and blessed is the fruit of thy womb, Jesus.
Holy Mary, Mother of God, pray for us sinners, now and at the hour of our death. Amen.

The Glory Be (The Doxology)
Glory be to the Father, and to the Son, and to the Holy Spirit. As it was in the beginning, is now, and ever shall be, world without end. Amen.

Morning Offering
O Jesus, through the Immaculate Heart of Mary, I offer you my

prayers, works, joys, and sufferings of this day for all the intentions of your Sacred Heart, in union with the holy sacrifice of the Mass throughout the world, in thanksgiving for your favors, in reparation for my sins, for the intentions of all my relatives and friends, and in particular for the intentions of the Holy Father. Amen.

Prayer to One's Guardian Angel

Angel of God, my guardian dear, to whom God's love commits me here, ever this day (or night) be at my side, to light and guard, to rule and guide. Amen.

Healing Prayer

Jesus, I ask you to enter into my heart and release me from those life experiences that torment me. You know me so much better than I know myself. Therefore, bring your love to every corner of my heart. Wherever you discover the wounded child, touch, console and release me.

Walk back through my life to the very moment when I was conceived. Cleanse my bloodlines and free me from those things which may have exerted a negative influence at that moment. Bless me again as I was being formed within my mother's womb and remove all barriers to wholeness which may have affected me during those months of confinement. Bridge the gap between the love that I needed and never perceived receiving.

Jesus, I ask you to surround my infancy with your light and heal those memories which keep me from being free. If I needed more of a mother's love, send me your Mother, Mary, to provide whatever was lacking. If I needed more of a father's love and security to assure me that I was wanted and loved very deeply, I ask you to hold me and let me feel your strong, protective arms. Give me renewed confidence and courage to face the trials of the world because I know my Father's love will support me if I stumble and fall.

Thank you, Lord!

Prayer to Break the Inner Vow

I break this inner vow of _____. I speak directly to the inner child and I say in Jesus' name I release you from this habit of _____. I restore you to the original delight of the person created by our Lord, Jesus Christ. I release you in Jesus' name to be the person fully alive to the work of the Holy Spirit.

Thank you Jesus, that you will continue to assist me with this predicament, and bring Freedom of Spirit instead. Amen.

Freedom from Manipulation

I renounce and reject all my ways of controlling people, Lord. I'm sorry for it, I cast it away from me. Help me every time I fall back into it. I detest it. Wherein I don't hate it enough, create in me a perfect hatred of this attitude which makes me a destroyer of my friends and loved ones. Thank you, Jesus. Amen.

Healing Prayer at Bedtime

Jesus, through the power of the Holy Spirit I release to you my memory as I sleep. Every hurt that has ever been done to me, heal that hurt.

Every hurt that I have ever caused to another person, heal that hurt. All the relationships that hve been damaged in my whole life and I have buried deep within me, please heal those relationships.

Jesus, if there is anything that I need to do, if I need to go to anyone, because they are still suffering from my attitude, bring that person to my awareness.

I choose to forgive by the power of the Holy Spirit dwelling within me, and I ask to be forgiven. Remove whatever bitterness or behavior pattern that I have developed as a result of my attitude of unforgiveness. Forgive me Jesus, for the times that I did not want to forgive.

Jesus, please fill the empty spaces with your love. Thank you, Jesus. Amen.

Prayer in Time of Sickness

O Jesus, you suffered and died for us; you understand suffering. Teach me to understnad my suffering as you do; to bear it in union with you; to offer it with you to atone for my sins and to bring your grace to souls in need.

Calm my fears; increase my trust. May I gladly accept your holy will and become more like you in trial. If it be your will, restore me to health so that I may work for your honor and glory and the salvation of others. Amen.

Mary, help of the sick, pray for me.

Prayer for the Sick

Jesus, Divine Physician and Healer of the sick, we turn to you in this time of illness. Comforter of the troubled, alleviate our worry and sorrow with your gentle love, and grant us the grace and strength to accept this burden. Dear God, we place our worries in your hands. We place our sick under your care and humbly ask that you restore your servant to health again. Above all, grant us the grace to acknowledge your holy will and know that whatsoever you do, you do for the love of us. Amen.

Prayer in Time of Suffering

Behold me, my beloved Jesus, weighed down under the burden of my trials and sufferings. I cast myself at your feet, that you may renew my strength and my courage. Permit me to lay down my cross in your Sacred Heart, for only your infinite goodness can sustain me; only your love can help me bear this cross. O Divine King, Jesus, whose heart is so compassionate to the afflicted, I wish to live in you; suffer and die in you. During my life, be my model and support; at the hour of death, be my hope and refuge.

Prayer for a Happy Death

O glorious St. Joseph, I choose you today for my special patron in life and at the hour of my death. Increase in me the spirit of prayer and fervor in the service of God. Remove far from me every kind of sin; obtain for me that my death may not come unawares, but that I may have time to confess my sins sacramentally and be truly sorry for them, so that I may breathe forth my soul into the hands of Jesus and Mary. Amen.

Prayer for the Dying

Most Merciful Jesus, I pray that, by the agony of your Sacred Heart and by the sorrows of your Immacualte Mother, you be with those who are in their last suffering and will die today. Heart of Jesus, once in agony, have mercy on the dying.

Prayer for Those Who Have Died

Lord God, to your mercy we owe our forgiveness and salvation. Grant that your servant [name] who has departed from this life, may be admitted into everlasting happiness through the intercession of the Blessed Virgin Mary and all your saints.

Prayer for the Unborn

Heavenly Father, you create us in your own image and you desire that not even the least among us should perish. In your love for us, you entrusted your only Son to the holy Virgin Mary. Now, in your love, protect the unborn to whom you have given the gift of life.

Prayer of St. Francis of Assisi

Lord, make me an instrument of your peace. Where there is hatred, let me sow love; where there is injury, pardon; where there is doubt, faith; where there is despair, hope; where there is darkness, light; and where there is sadness, joy.
O Divine Master, grant that I may not so much seek to be consoled as to console; to be understood as to understand; to be loved as to love. For it is in giving that we receive; it is in pardoning that we are pardoned; and it is in dying that we are born to eternal life.

Prayer to St. Michael

St. Michael, the Archangel, defend us in battle; be our defense against the wickedness and snares of the devil. May God rebuke him, we humbly pray, and do you, O Prince of the heavenly host, by the power of God, cast into hell Satan and the other evil spirits, who prowl about the world for the ruin of souls. Amen.

Prayer to St. Lucy
(Prayer for protection against eye ailments)

Relying on your goodness, O God, we humbly ask you, through the intercession of St. Lucy, Virgin and Martyr, to give perfect vision to our eyes, that they may serve for your greater honor and glory. St. Lucy, hear our prayers and obtain our petitions.

Prayer to St. Peregrine
(Patron saint of cancer patients)

O St. Peregrine, you who have been called "The Wonder-Worker" because of the numerous miracles which you have obtained from God for those who have had recourse to you, who for so many years bore in your own flesh this cancerous disease that destroys the very fiber of our being, and who had recourse to the source of all grace when the power of man could do no more; you who were favored with the vision of Jesus coming down from His Cross to heal your affliction, ask of God and Our Lady the cure of these sick persons whom we entrust to you [names of those for whom you are praying]. Aided in this way by your powerful intercession, we shall praise God for His great goodness and mercy. Amen.

Prayers to St. Gerard
(Prayer for motherhood)

St. Gerard, powerful intercessor before God and wonder-worker of our day, I call upon you and seek your aid. You, who on earth always fulfilled God's design, help me to do the Holy Will of God. Beseech the Master of Life, from Whom all paternity proceeds, to render me fruitful in offspring, that I may raise up children to God in this life and heirs to the Kingdom of His glory in the world to come. Amen.

Prayer for an Expectant Mother
Great St. Gerard, beloved servant of Jesus Christ, perfect imitator of Jesus, and devoted child of the Mother of God, enkindle within my heart one spark of that heavenly fire of charity which glowed in yours. Becuase you bore without murmur or complaint the calumnies of wicked men when falsely accused of crime, you have been raised up by God as the patron and protector of expectant mothers. Preserve me in the dangers of motherhood and shield the child I now bear, that it may be brought safely to the light of day and receive the sacrament of baptism.

Prayer to St. Dymphna
(For the mentally afflicted)
O God, we humbly beseech you through your servant, St. Dymphna, who sealed with her blood the love she bore you, to grant relief to those who suffer from mental afflictions and nervous disorders, especially [name]. St. Dymphna, helper of the mentally afflicted, pray for us!
(Glory Be three times)

Daily Prayer to St. Jude
O glorious Apostle, St. Jude, true relative of Jesus and Mary, I salute you through the Most Sacred Heart of Jesus.
I praise and thank God for all the graces he has bestowed upon you. I implore you, through the Sacred Heart of Jesus, to look upon me with compassion. Despise not my poor prayer and let not my trust be in vain. To you has been assigned the privilege of aiding mankind in the most desperate cases. Come to my aid that I may praise the mercies of God.

All my life, I will be grateful to you and will be your faithful client until I can thank you in heaven. Amen.

"Breastplate" Prayer of St. Patrick

Christ be with; Christ within me.
Christ behind me; Christ before me.
Christ beside me; Christ to win me.
Christ to comfort and restore me.
Christ beneath me; Christ above me.
Christ in quiet; Christ in danger.
Christ in the hearts of all who love me.
Christ in mouth of friend and stranger.

Prayer for a Family

O Jesus, I humbly implore you to grant your special graces to our family. May our home be a shrine of peace, purity, love, labor, and faith. I beg you, Jesus, to protect and bless all of us, absent and present, living and dead.

O Mary, loving Mother of Jesus, and our Mother, pray to Jesus for our family, for all the families of the world, to guard the cradle of the newborn, the schools of the young, and their vocations.

Blessed St. Joseph, holy guardian of Jesus and Mary, assist us by your prayers in all the necessities of life. Ask of Jesus that special grace which he granted to you, to watch over our home at the bed of the sick and dying, so that with Mary and with you, heaven may find our family unbroken in the Sacred Heart of Jesus. Amen.

Prayer for a Household

Hear us, Lord, and send your angel from heaven to visit and protect, to comfort and defend all who live in this house. Amen.

For Sanctification of One's Work

Lord God, by the labor of men and women, you govern and guide to perfection the work of creation. Hear our prayers and give all people work that enhances their human dignity and draws them closer to each other in the service of their brothers and sisters.

For Any Need
God, our Father, our strength in adversity, our health in weakness, our comfort in sorrow, be merciful to your people. As you have given us the punishment we deserve, give us also new life and hope as we rest in your kindness.

Serenity Prayer
Lord God, grant me the *serenity* to accept the things I cannot change; *courage* to change the things I can; *wisdom* to know the difference.

Prayer of Thanksgiving
Lord God, your gifts of love are countless and your goodness is infinite. From your hand, we have received generous gifts so that we might learn to share your blessings with others in gratitude. We come to you with gratitude for your kindness. Open our hearts to concern for others, so that we may share your gifts in loving service to them.

Prayer Before a Crucifix
Good and gentle, Jesus, I kneel before you. I see and I ponder your five wounds. My eyes behold what David prophesied about you: "They have pierced my hands and feet; they have counted all my bones."
Engrave on me this image of yourself. Fulfill the yearnings of my heart: give me faith, hope and love, repentance for my sins, and true conversion of life. Amen.

Prayer Before Confession
Come, Holy Spirit, into my soul.
Enlighten my mind that I may know the sins I ought to confess, and grant me your grace to confess them fully, humbly, and with

contrite heart. Help me to firmly resolve not to commit them again. O Blessed Virgin, Mother of my Redeemer, mirror of innocense and sanctity, and refuge of penitent sinners, intercede for me through the Passion of your Son, that I may obtain the grace to make a good confession.

All you blessed angels and saints of God, pray for me, a sinner, that I may repent from my sinful ways, that my heart may henceforth be forever united with yours in eternal love. Amen.

Act of Contrition

O my God, I am heartily sorry for having offended you, and I detest all my sins, because I dread the loss of heaven and the pains of hell; but most of all because they offend you, my God, who are all good and deserving of all my love. I firmly resolve, with the help of your grace, to confess my sins, to do penance, and to amend my life. Amen.

Prayer After Confession

Lord Jesus, I have confessed my sins to the best of my ability. I have sincerely tried to make a good confession and I know that you have forgive me. Thank you, Jesus!

Your divine heart is full of love and mercy for sinners. I love you, Jesus; you are so good to me.

My loving Savior, I shall try to keep from sin and to love you more each day.

Dearest Mother Mary, pray for me and help me to keep all of my promises. Protect me and do not let me fall back into sin.

Dear God, help me to lead a good life. Without your grace, I can do nothing. Amen.

Spiritual Communion

(When unable to receive Holy Communion, it is a pious practice to make a Spiritual Communion, praying the following prayer of St. Francis.)

I believe that you, O Jesus, are in the most holy Sacrament. I love you and desire you. Come into my heart. I embrace you. Oh, never leave me. I beseech you, Lord Jesus Christ, to absorb my mind that I may die through love of your love, who were graciously pleased to die through love of my love.

Readers who would like to share their personal stories of healing may send them to:
Father Larry Gesy
c/o Catholic Healing Ministry of Baltimore
4414 Wilkens Avenue
Baltimore, MD 21229
Those sent will be considered for inclusion in a future book of healing stories.